From our Kitchen to Yours

ALL-TIME-FAVORITE RECIPES
From

SOUTHERN
California
COOKS

Dedication

For every cook who wants to create amazing
recipes from the great cooks of
Southern California.

Appreciation

Thanks to all our Southern California cooks who
shared their delightful and delicious recipes with us!

Gooseberry Patch
An imprint of Globe Pequot
246 Goose Lane
Guilford, CT 06437
www.gooseberrypatch.com
1 800 854 6673

Copyright 2019, Gooseberry Patch
978-1-62093-344-2

Do you have a tried & true recipe... tip, craft or
memory that you'd like to see featured in a
Gooseberry Patch cookbook? Visit our website at
www.gooseberrypatch.com and follow the easy steps
to submit your favorite family recipe.

Or send them to us at:

Gooseberry Patch
PO Box 812
Columbus, OH 43216-0812

Don't forget to include the number of servings your
recipe makes, plus your name, address, phone
number and email address. If we select your recipe,
your name will appear right along with it... and you'll
receive a FREE copy of the book!

Southern California COOKS

THE GOLDEN STATE

Southern California, identified by its laid-back, casual lifestyle, is a mecca for innovative foods. With its mix of desert, mountain, farm fields and beach terrains, this part of the Golden State is rich in growing foods and creating iconic dishes.

Agriculture is huge in this area. Farms produce dairy and beef cattle and poultry. Numerous fruits and veggies come from farms, including avocados, grapes, peaches, pears, oranges, olives, apricots, figs, nectarines. melons, plums, prunes, almonds and walnuts. Plus, there are artichokes, Brussels sprouts, garlic, asparagus, broccoli, carrots, onions, and lettuce fields. Hay, rice, barley, sugar beets and wheat add to the economy.

In like manner, the fishing industry includes tuna, anchovies, flounder, salmon, sea bass, swordfish, abalones, crabs, shrimp, squid and oysters. Food-wise, choices are deeply influenced by the proximity to Mexico and the influx of numerous Asian cultures.

In this Gooseberry Patch cookbook, the talented cooks from the Golden State share their recipes that are dear to their hearts. You'll find everything from a Fresh Herb Quiche and Quinoa Stuffed Peppers to Take-It-Easy Tortellini Soup and Chicken Taco Salad. We know you will love this collection of recipes from these amazing cooks from beautiful Southern California.

OUR STORY

Back in 1984, our families were neighbors in little Delaware, Ohio. With small children, we wanted to do what we loved and stay home with the kids too. We had always shared a love of home cooking and so, **Gooseberry Patch** was born.

Almost immediately, we found a connection with our customers and it wasn't long before these friends started sharing recipes. Since then we've enjoyed publishing hundreds of cookbooks with your tried & true recipes.

We know we couldn't have done it without our friends all across the country and we look forward to continuing to build a community with you. Welcome to the **Gooseberry Patch** family!

JoAnn & Vickie

TABLE OF CONTENTS

CHAPTER ONE

GOOD-TO-GO

Breakfast & Brunch

THE SUNSHINE IS CALLING AND
YOU WILL BE READY TO ENJOY
EVERY MINUTE WHEN YOU SERVE
THESE BRIGHTEN-YOUR-DAY
DISHES FOR A GOOD-MORNING
BREAKFAST OR BRUNCH.

ALL-DAY APPLE BUTTER

CHERYL VOLBRUCK
COSTA MESA, CA

A slow-cooker favorite! One taste of this apple butter on a warm biscuit or in a bowl of oatmeal and you won't be eating any other apple butter again!

3-1/2 lbs. Pippin apples, peeled, cored and sliced

2 lbs. Granny Smith apples, peeled, cored and sliced

2 c. sugar

2 c. brown sugar, packed

2 t. cinnamon

1/4 t. ground cloves

1/4 t. salt

1/8 t. nutmeg

6 1/2-pint canning jars and lids, sterilized

1 Place all ingredients in a large slow cooker. Stir to mix well. Cover and cook on high setting for one hour. Reduce heat to low setting and cook 9 to 11 hours more, stirring occasionally, until mixture is thick and dark brown.

2 Uncover; cook one hour longer. Ladle hot butter into hot sterilized jars, leaving 1/4-inch headspace. Wipe rims; secure with lids and rings. Process in a boiling-water bath for 10 minutes. Set jars on a towel to cool; check for seals.

Makes 5 to 6 jars

BONUS IDEA

An old secret for the flakiest biscuits! Just stir to moisten and gently roll or pat the dough. Don't overmix it.

AUTUMN HERB BREAD

SHARON VELENOSI
COSTA MESA, CA

The bread is packed with the flavors of fall! I bake it before Thanksgiving so we can use it for turkey sandwiches. If you don't have these herbs on hand, you can substitute 1-3/4 teaspoons poultry seasoning.

1 In a large bowl, combine yeast, warm water and one tablespoon sugar or honey. Let stand until yeast is softened. Add milk, remaining sugar or honey, salt, butter, eggs and 2 cups flour to yeast mixture. Mix well. Cover and let rise in a warm place for about one hour, until bubbly.

2 Combine herbs and add to mixture. Stir in enough of remaining flour to make a stiff dough. Knead dough on a floured surface until satiny and elastic. Place in a large greased bowl, turning once to bring greased side up. Cover and let rise in warm place until double in size.

3 Punch down bread dough and let rise another 10 minutes. Shape dough into 2 loaves; place in 2 greased 9"x5" loaf pans. Brush tops with milk. Let rise for about 45 minutes, until well rounded at center and sides of dough reach the top of the pans. Bake at 375 degrees for 50 minutes, or until a toothpick comes out clean.

Makes 2 loaves

1 env. active dry yeast

1/4 c. very warm water, 110 to 115 degrees

1/4 c. sugar or honey, divided

1-1/2 c. warm milk

1 T. salt

1/2 c. butter, melted

3 eggs, beaten

6 to 7 c. all-purpose flour, divided

3/4 t. dried thyme

1 t. dried sage

3/4 t. dried marjoram

Garnish: additional milk

CALIFORNIA BREAKFAST CASSEROLE

**SANDY PERRY
BAKERSFIELD, CA**

This is an easy crowd-pleaser! It's a great way to use up leftover baked potatoes...don't be tempted to use frozen potatoes in this recipe. My whole family loves this one and they request it often.

1 doz. eggs, lightly beaten

2-1/2 c. shredded Cheddar cheese, divided

1 c. whipping cream

1 green pepper, chopped

1/2 c. onion, chopped

2 baked potatoes, peeled and chopped

salt and pepper to taste

1 lb. bacon, ground pork sausage or ham, cooked

Garnish: sour cream, salsa

1 Pour eggs into a greased 13"x9" baking pan. Sprinkle with one cup cheese; pour cream over top. Layer with remaining ingredients except garnish, ending with remaining cheese. Do not stir.

2 Bake, uncovered, at 350 degrees for 50 to 60 minutes. Let stand for 5 minutes; cut into squares. Serve topped with sour cream and salsa.

Makes 8 to 10 servings

CRANBERRY CHUTNEY

CALLA ANDREWS
LONG BEACH, CA

So good, we eat it with everything!

1 Bring cranberries, sugar and water to a boil in heavy 3-quart saucepan, stirring often; reduce heat and simmer 15 minutes. Stir in remaining ingredients; remove from heat. Ladle into sterilized jars; secure with lids. Refrigerate up to 3 weeks.

Makes 6 jars

16-oz. pkg. cranberries
2 c. sugar
1 c. water
1 T. orange zest
1 c. orange juice
1 c. raisins
1 c. celery, diced
1 apple, cored, peeled and minced
1 T. whole ginger, minced
6 1/2-pint canning jars and lids, sterilized

CALIFORNIA COOL

One of the most popular dishes in Southern California is avocado toast, a way to celebrate one of the state's prolific crops. It's guacamole on toast, sometimes topped with caviar, feta cheese, radishes or as is. Best to eat it with a knife and fork.

DENVER OVEN OMELET

CHARLENE MCCAIN
BAKERSFIELD, CA

Delicious and easy! I have taken this simple dish to many breakfast potlucks, since it bakes while I get ready for work. My family even enjoys it on Christmas morning after we've opened our presents. Even though it has Denver in the name, we love it in California!

8 eggs, beaten
1/2 c. half-and-half
1 c. shredded Cheddar cheese
1 c. cooked ham, chopped
1/4 c. green pepper, chopped
1/4 c. onion, finely chopped
salt and pepper to taste

1 In a large bowl, whisk eggs and half-and-half until light and fluffy. Stir in remaining ingredients.

2 Pour into a greased 9"x9" baking pan. Bake, uncovered, at 350 degrees for about 45 minutes or until set.

Serves 8

PARMESAN PULL-APARTS

BARBARA STURM
BAKERSFIELD, CA

Recruit your kids to roll the dough balls. They'll have fun both making and eating these yummy rolls.

3 T. butter
1 t. sesame seed
1/2 t. celery seed
1 T. dried, minced onion
10-oz. tube refrigerated flaky biscuits, quartered
1/4 c. grated Parmesan cheese

1 In a 400-degree oven, melt butter in a 9" round cake pan. Remove pan from oven; sprinkle seeds and onion evenly over butter. Meanwhile, roll biscuit pieces into balls; place in a large plastic zipping bag. Add cheese; shake to coat. Arrange dough balls evenly in pan. Sprinkle with any remaining cheese from bag. Bake at 400 degrees for 15 to 18 minutes, until golden.

Makes 10 servings

FRESH FRUIT WITH CREAMY SAUCE

SONYA LABBE
SANTA MONICA, CA

You can make this dish using many different fruits depending on what's in season.

1 Stir together yogurt, applesauce and honey; set aside. Toss together fruit in a large bowl; divide among 6 dessert dishes. Spoon sauce over top.

Serves 6

1/2 c. vanilla yogurt
1/4 c. unsweetened applesauce
2 t. honey
1 c. apples, cored and sliced
1 c. oranges, peeled and sliced
1 c. strawberries, hulled
1 c. blueberries
1 c. raspberries
1 banana, peeled and sliced
1/2 c. seedless grapes

SCRAMBLED EGG IN A CUP

LISA SETT
THOUSAND OAKS, CA

This is my favorite "breakfast on the go" before I go to the gym. Comes out perfect every time! Easy for older kids to make for themselves...try it on an English muffin.

1 Beat egg, salt and pepper well in a greased microwave-safe mug; add spinach. Microwave on high for one minute. Garnish as desired and serve from mug.

Serves one

1 egg
salt and pepper to taste
2 T. fresh spinach, chopped
Garnish: 1 to 2 t. shredded cheese, salsa, sliced green onion

FRESH HERB QUICHE

SONYA LABBE
LOS ANGELES, CA

This delicious quiche recipe has been in my family for generations. I couldn't wait to get home from school to eat it. It is always a hit at brunch or dinner. Add your own favorite garden herbs...scrumptious!

9-inch pie crust
1/2 c. shredded mozzarella cheese
1/2 c. shredded Swiss cheese
1/2 c. shredded Gruyère cheese
1/2 c. crumbled goat cheese or feta cheese
5 eggs, beaten
1 c. half-and-half
1 T. fresh dill
1 T. fresh parsley
1 T. fresh basil

1 Arrange crust in a 9" quiche pan or pie plate. Fill with shredded cheeses; set aside. In a blender, combine crumbled cheese and remaining ingredients. Process on high speed for 2 minutes, until smooth. Pour over cheeses in crust.

2 Bake at 400 degrees for 45 minutes, or until a knife inserted in the center tests clean. Cool for 5 minutes; cut into wedges.

Serves 4 to 6

BONUS IDEA

Use a muffin tin in place of individual casserole dishes when making mini pot pies, quiches or savory popovers. So quick & easy!

PUMPKIN STREUSEL MUFFINS

ELIZABETH CISNEROS
EASTVALE, CA

The best thing about fall...pumpkin goodies are everywhere! I like to use pumpkin as often as possible. This recipe can also be used to make loaves of pumpkin bread, which freeze beautifully.

1 Combine sugar, applesauce, oil and eggs in a bowl. Beat with an electric mixer on low speed until blended; beat in pumpkin and water. In a separate bowl, whisk together flour, baking soda, salt and spices. Add flour mixture slowly to pumpkin mixture; beat on low speed just until moistened and smooth. Stir in nuts.

2 Fill paper-lined muffin cups 2/3 full. Sprinkle with Streusel Topping. Bake at 350 degrees for 30 to 35 minutes, until a toothpick tests clean. Batter may also be divided between 2 greased 9"x5" loaf pans; add topping and bake for about one hour.

Makes 2 dozen muffins or 2 loaves

3 c. sugar
1/2 c. applesauce
1/2 c. canola oil
4 eggs
2 c. canned pumpkin
2/3 c. water
3-1/3 c. all-purpose flour
2 t. baking soda
1-1/2 t. salt
1-1/2 t. cinnamon
1 t. nutmeg
1 c. chopped pecans

1 Combine all ingredients; mix with a fork until crumbly.

STREUSEL TOPPING:
1/3 c. brown sugar, packed
2 T. butter, room temperature
1/2 t. cinnamon
1/4 c. finely chopped pecans

HASHBROWN QUICHE

SANDY PERRY
BAKERSFIELD, CA

I had something like this once at a B&B while on a road trip. Makes a very nice breakfast when served with a basket of warm scones and a cup of fresh fruit.

24-oz. pkg frozen shredded hashbrown potatoes, thawed and patted dry
1/3 c. butter, melted
1 c. cooked ham, diced
1 c. shredded Pepper Jack cheese
2 eggs, beaten
1/2 c. milk
1/4 t. seasoned salt

1 Spray a 9" pie plate with non-stick vegetable spray. Press potatoes into pan to form a crust; brush potatoes with melted butter. Bake at 425 degrees for 25 minutes. Remove from oven. Layer ham and cheese in crust; set aside.

2 Whisk together eggs, milk and salt in a bowl; pour over cheese. Bake at 425 degrees for 30 to 40 minutes, until set and golden.

Serves 6 to 8

GRANNY JUDY'S GRANOLA

JUDY BORECKY
ESCONDIDO, CA

After I sampled a fabulous granola at a restaurant in my area, I tried to copy the recipe at home. I think I came pretty close...it's delicious! The cranberries stay soft because they're added to the already-baked granola.

3 c. old-fashioned oats, uncooked
3 c. pecan halves
2 c. flaked coconut
14-oz. sweetened condensed milk
1/2 c. butter, melted
1/2 t. salt
1 c. sweetened dried cranberries

1 In a large bowl, combine all ingredients except cranberries; stir until blended. Spread on a 15"x10" jelly-roll pan that has been sprayed with non-stick vegetable spray. Bake at 250 degrees for 90 minutes, stirring after one hour. Remove from oven; add cranberries. Cool completely; store in an airtight container.

Makes about 9 cups

CLOVERLEAF ROLLS

KATHY SCHROEDER
RIVERSIDE, CA

I usually double this recipe and freeze any extra rolls. These are great for breakfast, warmed in the microwave with homemade fresh strawberry jam!

1 In large bowl, combine one cup of flour, sugar, salt and yeast. In medium saucepan over low heat, heat water, milk and 1/4 cup butter until very warm. With an electric mixer at low speed, gradually pour liquid into dry ingredients. Increase speed to medium; beat 2 minutes, occasionally scraping bowl with rubber spatula. Beat in eggs and enough flour to make a thick batter. Continue beating 2 minutes, occasionally scraping bowl. With spoon, stir in enough additional flour to make a soft dough.

2 Turn dough onto lightly floured surface and knead for 10 minutes or until dough is smooth and elastic. Shape dough into ball and place in a large greased bowl, turning over so that top of dough is greased.

3 Cover with towel; let rise in warm place, away from drafts, for one hour or until doubled. Punch down dough by pushing down the center of dough, then push edges of dough into center. Turn dough onto lightly floured surface; cut in half. Cover with towel for 15 minutes. Grease 24, 2 to 3-inch muffin cups.

4 With sharp knife or kitchen shears, cut one-half of dough into 36 equal pieces. Shape each piece into a smooth ball. Place 3 balls into each muffin cup. Brush tops with remaining melted butter. Cover with towel; let rise in warm place for 45 minutes or until doubled. Repeat with second half of dough. Uncover rolls. Bake at 400 degrees for 10 to 15 minutes, until golden. Remove from pan.

Makes 24 rolls

4 to 5 c. all-purpose
   flour, divided
1/3 c. sugar
1 t. salt
2 envs. instant dry yeast
1/2 c. water
1/2 c. milk
1/2 c. butter, melted and
   divided
2 eggs

KOFFEE KLATCH
OATMEAL MUFFINS

SHARON VELENOSI
COSTA MESA, CA

Great to serve with coffee for the neighborhood ladies after the kids are off to school. Sometimes I'll use maple sugar for a touch of fall instead of brown sugar.

1 c. long-cooking oats, uncooked
1 c. buttermilk
1 c. all-purpose flour
1 t. baking powder
1/2 t. baking soda
1/2 t. salt
1/3 c. butter, softened
1/2 c. brown sugar, packed
1 egg
3/4 to 1 c. raisins

1 Combine oats and buttermilk in a bowl; let stand for one hour. In a bowl, mix together flour, baking powder, baking soda and salt. In a separate large bowl, whisk together butter, brown sugar and egg. Add flour mixture and oat mixture to butter mixture; stir well but do not overbeat. Fold in raisins.

2 Spoon batter into 12 well-greased muffin cups, filling 2/3 full. Bake at 400 degrees for 20 to 25 minutes.

Makes one dozen

LIGHTER-THAN-AIR POTATO ROLLS

LINDA CUELLAR
RIVERSIDE, CA

These are wonderful right out of the oven served with butter, jam, apple butter or honey.

1 In a bowl, stir together potato flakes, sugar, butter and hot water. Add cold water and baking mix; stir until a soft dough forms. Gently form dough into a ball on a floured surface; knead 8 to 10 times. Roll out into a 10-inch by 6-inch rectangle. Cut into 12 squares; arrange on an ungreased baking sheet. Bake at 450 degrees for about 10 minutes, or until golden.

Makes one dozen

1/2 c. instant mashed potato flakes
1 t. sugar
2 T. butter, softened
1/2 c. hot water
1/3 c. cold water
2 c. biscuit baking mix

POACHED EGGS & GRITS

PAMELA STUMP
CHINO HILLS, CA

I live in California now, but being raised down south, for me nothing beats poached eggs and grits...one of my ultimate comfort foods!

1 Combine water and salt in a medium saucepan over high heat; bring to a boil. Gradually whisk in grits. Reduce heat to low. Cover and cook, whisking often, until thick and creamy. Stir in remaining ingredients except eggs; cook 5 minutes longer.

2 Meanwhile, to poach eggs, add 2 inches water to a skillet. Bring to a simmer over high heat. Break eggs into a cup, one at a time, and slide into simmering water. Cook eggs for 3 minutes. To serve, spoon grits into 4 bowls. With a slotted spoon, top each bowl with 2 eggs.

Serves 4

5-1/2 c. water
1/2 t. salt
1-1/2 c. quick-cooking grits, uncooked
2 T. butter
1/3 c. finely shredded Parmigiano Reggiano cheese
1/4 c. green onions, finely chopped
4 slices bacon, crisply cooked and crumbled
pepper to taste
8 eggs

MAKE-AHEAD BREAKFAST CASSEROLE

BARBARA HUNTER STURM
BAKERSFIELD, CA

For a fuss-free morning, assemble the evening before, then just pop into the oven in the morning.

6-oz. pkg. seasoned croutons
1 lb. bacon, crisply cooked and crumbled
1-1/2 to 2 c. shredded Cheddar cheese
1 doz. eggs, beaten
1/2 c. half-and-half or milk
salt and pepper to taste

1 Spray a 13"x9" baking pan with non-stick vegetable spray. Arrange croutons in bottom of pan. Layer with bacon and cheese. In a bowl, beat together eggs, half-and-half or milk, salt and pepper. Pour egg mixture evenly over cheese. Cover and refrigerate overnight. Bake, uncovered, at 350 degrees for 35 minutes, or until heated through and eggs are fluffy.

Serves 6 to 8

BAKED EGGS IN TOMATOES

JILL BURTON
GOOSEBERRY PATCH

So pretty for a brunch...a delicious way to enjoy tomatoes from the farmers' market.

6 tomatoes, tops cut off
1/4 t. pepper
1/2 c. corn, thawed if frozen
1/2 c. red pepper, diced
1/2 c. mushrooms, diced
2 T. cream cheese, softened and divided
6 eggs
2 t. fresh chives, minced
1/4 c. grated Parmesan cheese

1 With a spoon, carefully scoop out each tomato, creating shells. Sprinkle pepper inside tomatoes. Divide corn, red pepper and mushrooms among tomatoes; top each with one teaspoon cream cheese. In a bowl, whisk together eggs and chives. Divide egg mixture among tomatoes; top with Parmesan cheese. Place filled tomatoes in a lightly greased 2-quart casserole dish.

2 Bake, uncovered, at 350 degrees until egg mixture is set, about 45 to 50 minutes. Serve warm.

Makes 6 servings

SNICKERDOODLE SCONES

CHARMIE FISHER
FONTANA, CA

Such yummy scones! I created this recipe because of my husband's love of the snickerdoodle cookies his grandma used to make. These scones are a new twist that bring back pleasant memories for him.

1 Combine sour cream and baking soda in a small bowl; set aside. Combine flour, sugar, baking powder, cream of tartar and salt. Cut in butter until mixture resembles fine bread crumbs. Whisk egg and cinnamon into sour cream mixture; add to flour mixture and stir until just moistened.

2 Gather dough into a ball and place on a baking sheet sprayed with non-stick vegetable spray. Pat into a circle, 3/4-inch thick. Cut into 8 wedges and separate slightly on baking sheet. Dust with sugar and cinnamon. Bake at 350 degrees for 15 to 20 minutes, until golden.

Makes 8 scones

1/2 c. sour cream
1/2 t. baking soda
2 c. all-purpose flour
1/2 c. sugar
1 t. baking powder
1/8 t. cream of tartar
1/2 t. salt
1/2 c. butter
1 egg, beaten
2 t. cinnamon
Garnish: additional
  sugar and cinnamon

BONUS IDEA

When recipes call for eggs, that usually refers to large eggs. Extra large eggs will yield more liquid in the recipe.

PEACHY OAT BREAD

**SHARON VELENOSI
COSTA MESA, CA**

*So yummy made with fresh peaches just off the tree! I've also used
canned peaches, drained very well.*

2 c. whole-wheat flour

1 c. quick-cooking oats,
uncooked

3/4 c. sugar

3 T. baking powder

1/2 t. baking soda

1/2 t. salt

1/2 t. cinnamon

2 c. peaches, pitted and
chopped

2 eggs, beaten

1 c. milk

1/4 c. oil

1 In a large bowl, stir together dry ingredients. Add peaches and stir gently to coat; set aside. In a separate bowl, whisk together eggs, milk and oil. Add to peach mixture; stir just until moistened.

2 Pour batter into a greased 9"x5" loaf pan. Bake at 350 degrees for one hour. Cool in pan 10 minutes. Remove from pan and cool completely on a wire rack.

Makes one loaf

CALIFORNIA COOL

Breakfast burritos are popular especially in San Diego, where meat, cheese, sour cream and even potatoes, combine for a tasty dish. Items like sushi rolls, quinoa granola and crab cakes from Dungeness crab from the Pacific Ocean, are tasty additions. Plus, in other parts of the country, brunch is a weekend popular meal choice. Here, brunch can take place everyday.

BREAKFAST BURRITOS

CARRIE O'SHEA
MARINA DEL REY, CA

A quick and hearty breakfast they will love!

1 Brown sausage in a skillet over medium heat; drain. Combine sausage, cheese and tomatoes in a bowl. Scramble eggs in same skillet. Add eggs to sausage mixture and mix thoroughly. Divide mixture evenly among tortillas and roll tightly. Seal tortillas by cooking for one to 2 minutes on a hot griddle sprayed with non-stick vegetable spray.

Serves 8

16-oz. pkg. ground pork breakfast sausage

8-oz. pkg. shredded Mexican-blend cheese

10-oz. can diced tomatoes with green chiles, drained

5 eggs, beaten

8 10-inch flour tortillas

SPINACH & EGG CASSEROLE

JILL WEISINGER
MURRIETA, CA

My mom used to make this dish for special occasions. I just loved it and would try to get her to serve it more often. It can be prepared the night before and just popped into the oven the next morning.

1 Place butter in a 9"x9"" baking pan; melt in a 350-degree oven. Mix remaining ingredients in a bowl; pour into pan. Bake, uncovered, at 350 degrees for 30 minutes, or until eggs are set.

Serves 6

2 T. butter

9 eggs, beaten

1/2 c. milk

1/2 c. sour cream

1 c. shredded Cheddar cheese

1-1/2 c. fresh baby spinach

salt and pepper to taste

CHAPTER TWO

FULL-OF-SUNSHINE

Salads, Sandwiches & Pizzas

WITH FRESH PRODUCE ALWAYS
NEARBY, IT IS A JOY TO MAKE
CALIFORNIA-STYLE SALADS,
SATISFYING SANDWICHES AND
TASTY PIZZAS THAT ARE SURE
TO PLEASE AND CARRY YOU
HAPPILY THROUGH YOUR DAY.

ARUGULA SALAD & BAKED PEARS

SONYA LABBE
WEST HOLLYWOOD, CA

This is a beautiful sweet and savory salad...my whole family loves it! Be sure to choose firm ripe pears.

3 Anjou pears, peeled and halved lengthwise

5 T. lemon juice

6 T. crumbled Gorgonzola cheese

1/4 c. sweetened dried cherries

1/4 c. pecan halves, toasted and chopped

1/2 c. apple cider

1/3 c. light brown sugar, packed

6-oz. pkg. arugula leaves

salt to taste

1 Core each pear half with a melon baller and a paring knife, creating a well. Trim bottoms of pear halves to sit flat. Drizzle pears with lemon juice and arrange, cored-side up, in an ungreased 8"x8" baking pan. In a small bowl, gently toss cheese, cherries and pecans together.

2 Divide cheese mixture among pears, mounding it in the wells. In the same bowl, combine cider and brown sugar; stir to dissolve sugar. Pour cider mixture over and around pears.

3 Bake, uncovered, at 375 degrees for 30 minutes, or until pears are tender, basting occasionally with cider mixture. Remove from oven, reserving cider mixture in pan; let stand until pears are warm or at room temperature. In a large bowl, add arugula to Dressing; toss well. Divide arugula mixture among 6 salad plates; top each with a pear half. Drizzle pears with some of the reserved cider mixture; sprinkle with salt and serve.

Makes 6 servings

DRESSING:
1/4 c. olive oil
1/4 c. lemon juice
1/4 c. reserved cider mixture

Whisk together ingredients.

BRATWURST & POTATO SALAD

**MYRON SCHIRER-SUTER
LOS ANGELES, CA**

Toasted, buttered dark rye bread goes well with this salad.

1 Cook bratwurst according to package instructions; brown in bacon drippings or oil. Cut into one-inch pieces.

2 Combine bratwurst, potatoes and green onions in a large bowl; set aside. Mix remaining ingredients together; pour over bratwurst mixture and toss to coat. Refrigerate overnight.

Serves 6 to 8

6 bratwurst
1/4 c. bacon drippings or oil
2 lbs. redskin potatoes, quartered and boiled
1 bunch green onions, thinly sliced
1/2 c. olive oil
3 T. white wine vinegar
2 T. German mustard
salt and pepper to taste
Optional: 1/8 t. sugar

CALIFORNIA COOL

Cobb Salad hit the California food scene in 1937, when Bob Cobb, who owned the Brown Derby restaurant, created the combination of salad greens, tomatoes, bacon, hard-boiled eggs, chicken, avocado and Roquefort or blue cheese dressing.

PEA SALAD

DEE FAULDING
SANTA BARBARA, CA

This is a great salad to bring to any summer gathering or a sunny picnic in the park!

1 c. elbow macaroni, cooked

3 slices bacon, crisply cooked and crumbled

1/2 c. green onion, chopped

2 c. frozen baby peas, thawed

1 c. mayonnaise

1/2 c. shredded Cheddar cheese

1 In a bowl, combine macaroni, bacon, green onions and peas. Stir in mayonnaise; cover and refrigerate for at least 2 hours. Sprinkle with cheese just before serving.

Serves 4 to 6

CALIFORNIA COOL

A popular sandwich classic, French Dip, was born in the Los Angeles area in the early 1900s. There's more than a little discrepancy as to whether it began at one of two restaurants, Philippe's or Cole's. It's usually served warm with roast beef, Swiss cheese and au jus.

SANDRA'S POMEGRANATE SALAD

SANDRA SMITH
LANCASTER, CA

Here in California, people have pomegranate trees in their yards, and we had three such trees at our old house. I also make pomegranate jelly and a pomegranate cordial, but this salad is my favorite.

1 Place arugula and pears in a large salad bowl; set aside. In a small bowl, whisk together lime juice, olive oil and mustard. Toss arugula and pears with just enough lime juice mixture to coat; season with salt and pepper.

2 Sprinkle salad with pomegranate seeds; add cheese and pecans, if using. Line 6 salad plates with lettuce leaves; place a serving of salad in the center of each.

Serves 6

2 bunches arugula, torn
2 ripe pears, halved, cored and cut into wedges
2 T. fresh lime juice
2 T. olive oil
1/2 t. Dijon mustard
salt and pepper to taste
seeds of 1 pomegranate
Optional: 1/2 c. crumbled feta cheese, 1/3 c. toasted chopped pecans
Garnish: Boston or Bibb lettuce leaves

FIGURE-FRIENDLY 3-BEAN SALAD

**CAROL JACOBS
ANAHEIM, CA**

Serve this flavorful salad in a chilled bowl.

2 14-1/2 oz. cans green beans, drained

14-1/2 oz. can yellow wax beans, drained

1-1/2 c. garbanzo beans, drained and rinsed

1 sweet onion, diced

1 green pepper, diced

1 red or yellow pepper, diced

1/4 c. balsamic vinegar

1/4 c. red wine vinegar

1/4 c. lemon juice

3 T. canola oil

1 t. sugar

1/2 t. pepper

1 Combine all beans and vegetables in a large serving bowl; set aside. In a separate bowl, whisk together remaining ingredients. Pour over vegetable mixture; toss to coat. Cover and refrigerate.

Makes 10 servings

BONUS IDEA

Serve up salad dressings in pint milk bottles or wine carafes...charming!

TASTY TURKEY BURGERS

KATHLEEN STURM
CORONA, CA

My family loves these turkey burgers! They are flavorful and never bland, like turkey burgers tend to be.

1 Combine turkey, soy sauce, catsup and garlic powder in a large bowl. Mix together and form into 4 to 6 patties. Grill burgers over medium-high heat for about 5 to 7 minutes on each side. Serve burgers on buns with desired condiments.

Serves 4 to 6

1 lb. ground turkey
1 T. soy sauce
1 T. catsup
1/4 t. garlic powder
4 to 6 hamburger buns, split
Garnish: favorite condiments

SEASIDE SALMON BUNS

SHARON VELENOSI
GARDEN GROVE, CA

We like to serve these yummy sandwiches on pretzel buns for a nice change of pace.

1 Mix salmon, pepper, onion, lemon juice and mayonnaise. Pile salmon mixture onto bottom bun halves; sprinkle with cheese.

2 Arrange salmon-topped buns on an ungreased baking sheet. Broil until lightly golden and cheese is melted. Top with remaining bun halves.

Makes 6 servings

14-oz. can salmon, drained and flaked
1/4 c. green pepper, chopped
1 T. onion, chopped
2 t. lemon juice
1/2 c. mayonnaise
6 pretzel buns, split
1/2 c. shredded Cheddar cheese

TOMATO-BASIL COUSCOUS SALAD

SONYA LABBE
LOS ANGELES, CA

Everyone seems to love this salad. I think it is the combination of the couscous, basil and tomatoes.

2 c. water

1-1/2 c. couscous, uncooked

1 c. tomatoes, chopped

1/4 c. fresh basil, thinly sliced

1/2 c. olive oil

1/3 c. balsamic vinegar

1/2 t. salt

1/4 t. pepper

1 In a saucepan over high heat, bring water to a boil. Stir in uncooked couscous; remove from heat. Cover and let stand for 5 minutes, until water is absorbed. Add remaining ingredients and toss to mix. Cover and chill for several hours to overnight.

Makes 6 servings

KITCHEN TIP

Save that lemon, lime or orange half after it's been juiced! Wrap it and store in the freezer, ready to grate whenever a recipe calls for fresh citrus zest.

VICTORY VEGGIE PIZZA

LINDA MCCANN
SIMI VALLEY, CA

For a little change, try using flavored cream cheese…chive & onion or roasted garlic would be tasty.

1 Spread out crescent rolls to cover the bottom of a greased 13"x9" baking pan; pinch seams together. Bake at 350 degrees for 7 to 8 minutes; set aside to cool.

2 Mix cream cheese, sour cream, mayonnaise and half the salad dressing mix, reserving the remainder for use in another recipe; spread over crust. Sprinkle with vegetables; top with cheese. Cover with plastic wrap, gently pressing toppings into dressing layer; refrigerate for 3 to 4 hours. Cut into squares to serve.

Makes 18 servings

8-oz. tube refrigerated crescent rolls

8-oz. pkg. cream cheese, softened

1/4 c. sour cream

1/3 c. mayonnaise

1-oz. pkg. ranch salad dressing mix

3/4 c. broccoli, chopped

3/4 c. cauliflower, chopped

3/4 c. carrots, chopped

3/4 c. green onions, chopped

3/4 c. green pepper, chopped

3/4 c. tomatoes, chopped

3/4 c. shredded Cheddar cheese

ZIPPY TOMATO-CAULIFLOWER TOSS

YVONNE VAN BRIMMER
APPLE VALLEY, CA

This is my yummy way to get my kids to eat fresh veggies. They love it with any kind of barbecued meat!

2 beefsteak tomatoes, cubed

2 c. cauliflower flowerets

1 red onion, sliced and separated into rings

2 t. Salad Herb Seasoning

salt to taste

1 c. zesty Italian salad dressing

1 Combine all vegetables in a large bowl. Sprinkle with Salad Herb Seasoning and salt. Drizzle with salad dressing and toss to mix. Cover and chill for one hour to overnight.

Serves 4 to 6

SALAD HERB SEASONING:

2 t. sesame seed

1 t. dried oregano

1 t. dried basil

1 t. dried rosemary

1 t. dried thyme

1 t. granulated garlic

1 t. salt

1/2 t. sugar

1 Combine all ingredients in a small jar and shake. Keep covered.

CHICKEN NOODLE BURGERS

JUDY BORECKY
ESCONDIDO, CA

This recipe is from my mother. She lived to see her great-great-grandchildren and her 100th birthday, bless her heart. Mother loved to cook and all 5 generations of our family love her noodle burgers!

1 Combine ground beef, soup, oats, egg, onion salt and pepper. Mix all until just blended and form into 6 patties.

2 Place patties in a skillet over medium-high heat. Add a little water to the skillet so patties will steam as they fry.

3 Meanwhile, make gravy in a separate skillet. Sauté mushrooms in butter until tender. Stir in flour, broth and half-and-half; cook until slightly thickened. Stir in mustard; add salt and pepper to taste. Serve gravy over noodle burgers.

Makes 6 servings

1-1/4 lbs. ground beef round

10-3/4 oz. can chicken noodle soup, drained

1/3 c. instant oats, uncooked

1 egg, beaten

onion salt and pepper to taste

1/2 lb. sliced mushrooms

1/4 c. butter

3 T. all-purpose flour

1 c. chicken broth

1 c. half-and-half

1 t. Dijon mustard

salt and pepper to taste

HAWAIIAN BBQ BEEF

REBECCA GONZALEZ
MORENO VALLEY, CA

My mom used to make this for special occasions like football parties and such! A slow cooker makes it a snap. If you don't have a really large slow cooker, the brisket and other ingredients could be halved between two 4 or 5-quart smaller slow cookers, same cooktime.

6 to 8-lb. beef brisket
20-oz. bottle Hawaiian barbecue sauce
16-oz. jar salsa
1.35-oz. pkg. onion soup mix
hoagie rolls, split

1 Spray an 8-quart slow cooker with non-stick vegetable spray; add brisket. Combine remaining ingredients in a bowl; mix well and spoon over brisket. Cover and cook on low setting for 6 to 8 hours, until brisket falls apart. Shred brisket; serve on hoagie rolls.

Makes 20 to 25 sandwiches

BONUS IDEA

Scoop out oranges or melon halves and fill with a fresh fruit salad. They make individual serving dishes that are very pretty for a bridal or baby shower.

HOMEMADE FRESH BASIL PESTO

PAMELA STUMP
CHINO HILLS, CA

My daughter and I experimented with making our own pesto...we think we've come up with just the right ingredients and consistency!

1 In a food processor, combine nuts, basil, cheese, garlic, salt and pepper. Process until mixed to a coarse texture.

2 Add olive oil slowly, processing constantly at high speed to desired consistency. Add pesto to hot pasta and toss to mix. Or, for a tasty bruschetta, spread pesto on slices of toasted bread and top with diced tomatoes.

Serves 4

3/4 c. pine nuts or chopped toasted walnuts

3 c. fresh basil, loosely packed

1 c. grated Parmesan cheese

4 cloves garlic, peeled

salt and pepper to taste

1/2 to 3/4 c. olive oil

cooked angel hair pasta, or sliced French bread and diced tomatoes

NORMA'S FUMI SALAD

NORMA CHAVIRA
WEST COVINA, CA

This Asian twist on coleslaw is a welcome change from the ordinary. The ramen noodles and almonds add a yummy crunch, while the seasoned rice vinegar provides a flavorful bite.

2 16-oz. pkgs. coleslaw
  mix
4 green onions, chopped
1 bunch cilantro, finely
  chopped
3-oz. pkg. ramen noodles
1/4 c. sliced almonds,
  toasted
1 T. toasted sesame
  seeds

1 In a bowl, combine coleslaw mix, green onions and cilantro; toss well.

2 Crush ramen noodles; discard seasoning packet. Just before serving, toss crushed noodles, almonds and sesame seed into coleslaw. Drizzle with Dressing; mix well until evenly coated.

Makes 18 to 20 servings

DRESSING:
1/2 c. oil
3 T. seasoned rice
  vinegar
2 T. sugar
1 t. salt
1/2 t. pepper

1 Whisk together all ingredients in a bowl.

PAT'S SPINACH SALAD WITH STRAWBERRIES

**SANDY PERRY
BAKERSFIELD, CA**

My good friend Pat invited me over for a quilt lesson and made the most wonderful salad for us that hot June day. I just had to have the recipe!

1 In a large salad bowl, combine spinach, strawberries and oranges. Pour Dressing lightly over salad; toss to mix. Sprinkle almonds on top.

Makes 6 to 8 servings

6-oz. pkg. fresh spinach, torn

2 c. strawberries, hulled and sliced

11-oz. can mandarin oranges, drained

1/2 c. sliced almonds

1 Combine all ingredients in a jar; shake until well blended.

DRESSING:

1/2 c. olive oil

2 T. lemon juice

2 T. sugar

1 t. brown mustard

salt and pepper to taste

KITCHEN TIP

Make extra dressing and keep in the refrigerator for a last-minute salad topper.

CREAMY AMBROSIA SALAD

AMBER CARLSON
IRVINE, CA

On busy mornings, I love having a big bowl of this sweet, healthy fruit salad ready for my family's breakfast. It only requires a handful of ingredients and takes just minutes to put together.

1/2 c. mayonnaise
1 c. plain or vanilla yogurt
30-oz. can fruit cocktail, drained
20-oz. can pineapple chunks, drained
5-oz. pkg. sweetened flaked coconut
1/2 c. raisins
1/2 c. chopped walnuts

1 In a large bowl, fold mayonnaise into yogurt. Stir in remaining ingredients. Cover and refrigerate for 2 hours, or until thoroughly chilled.

Makes 8 to 10 servings

CREAMY BASIL SALAD DRESSING

PAT MINNICH
EL CAJON, CA

I grow my own basil and love this recipe. The dressing is so flavorful you would never guess it's low in fat!

1 t. shallot, chopped
1 clove garlic, chopped
2/3 c. Greek yogurt
3 T. balsamic vinegar
1 T. lemon juice
3 T. olive oil
⁕1/2 c. dried basil — *fresh equiv.*
salt and pepper to taste

1 Place all ingredients except salt and pepper in a food processor or blender. Proccess until smooth. Season with salt and pepper. Keep refrigerated.

Makes about 1-1/2 cups

CHICKEN TACO SALAD

**ABBY SNAY
SAN FRANCISCO, CA**

Such a colorful and tasty taco lunch!

1 Microwave tortillas on high setting for one minute, or until softened. Press each tortilla into an ungreased muffin cup to form a bowl shape. Bake at 350 degrees for 10 minutes; cool.

2 Combine chicken, taco seasoning and water in a skillet over medium heat. Cook, stirring frequently, until blended, about 5 minutes. Divide lettuce among tortilla bowls. Top with chicken and other ingredients, garnishing with salsa.

Makes 8 servings

8 6-inch flour tortillas
2 c. cooked chicken breast, shredded
2 t. taco seasoning mix
1/2 c. water
2 c. lettuce, shredded
1/2 c. black beans, drained and rinsed
1 c. shredded Cheddar cheese
1/2 c. green onion, sliced
1/2 c. canned corn, drained
2-1/4 oz. can sliced black olives, drained
1/2 avocado, pitted, peeled and cubed
Garnish: fresh salsa

BONUS IDEA

Make extra taco shell holders and keep in a plastic container to have on hand for other salad recipes. They will keep in the freezer for up to 2 months.

GERMAN POTATO SALAD

**CALLA ANDREWS
LONG BEACH, CA**

*This recipe was one of my first cooking successes as a new bride.
My husband and his family raved over it!*

6 redskin potatoes

10 slices bacon, chopped

1 red onion, finely
chopped

4 t. all-purpose flour

1 T. sugar

salt and pepper to taste

1/2 c. cider vinegar

1/2 c. water

1/4 c. fresh parsley,
minced

1 t. celery seed

1 Steam potatoes until tender; cool and peel. Thinly slice potatoes and transfer to a large bowl. Cook bacon in a heavy skillet over medium heat until crisp. Add onion; cook one minute. Stir in flour and sugar. Season with salt and pepper; stir.

2 Mix together vinegar and water; pour over bacon mixture. Stir until thickened. Pour over potatoes. Stir in parsley and celery seed.

Serves 6 to 8

COBB SANDWICHES

**JOYCE CHIZAUSKIE
VACAVILLE, CA**

*If you don't have time to fry bacon, mix some bacon bits with the blue
cheese dressing.*

2 T. blue cheese salad
dressing

3 slices country-style
bread, toasted

4-oz. grilled boneless,
skinless chicken breast

1 leaf green leaf lettuce

2 slices tomato

3 slices avocado

1 slice red onion

3 slices bacon, crisply
cooked

1 Spread blue cheese dressing on one side of each slice of toasted bread. On the first slice of bread, place chicken breast on dressing; top with a second bread slice. Layer with lettuce, tomato, avocado, onion and bacon; top with remaining bread slice. Cut sandwich in quarters, securing each section with a toothpick.

Makes 4 sandwich wedges

DEEP-DISH SAUSAGE PIZZA

KATHLEEN STURM
CORONA, CA

Why go out to a pizza parlor, when you can feast on a hot, hearty pizza right from your own kitchen? It's chock-full of the great Italian flavors we love.

1 Press dough into the bottom and up the sides of a greased 13"x9" baking pan; set aside. In a large skillet, crumble sausage and cook until no longer pink; drain.

2 Sprinkle sausage over dough; top with mozzarella cheese. In the same skillet, sauté peppers until slightly tender. Stir in tomatoes and seasonings; spoon over pizza. Sprinkle with Parmesan cheese.

3 Bake pizzza, uncovered, at 350 degrees for 25 to 35 minutes, until crust is golden.

Makes 8 servings

16-oz. pkg. frozen bread dough, thawed
1 lb. sweet Italian pork sausage, casings removed
2 c. shredded mozzarella cheese
1 green pepper, diced
1 red pepper, diced
2 8-oz. can diced tomatoes, drained
3/4 t. dried oregano
1/2 t. salt
1/4 t. garlic powder
1/2 c. grated Parmesan cheese

CHAPTER THREE

SEASIDE

Soups & Sides

SERVE SOUL-SOOTHING BOWLS

OF GOODNESS AND FRESH

SIDES CALIFORNIA STYLE WHEN

YOU MAKE THEM USING THESE

NO-FUSS RECIPES.

BOHEMIAN SAUERKRAUT

NANCY SHARP
CHULA VISTA, CA

A lot of people don't like sauerkraut because of the bitterness. But you'll love this! From the Tesar family tradition.

- 32-oz. jar refrigerated sauerkraut
- 10-3/4 oz. can cream of chicken soup
- 1/4 c. brown sugar, packed
- 4 slices bacon, crisply cooked and crumbled
- 3 T. caraway seed

1 Rinse and drain sauerkraut in a colander; transfer to a saucepan. Add remaining ingredients; bring to a simmer over low heat. Cook for one hour, stirring every 10 minutes or so.

Makes 6 servings

COLLINS' BEST LENTIL SOUP

MICHELLE COLLINS
SAN DIEGO, CA

Thanks to the hearty ingredients this soup offers, appetites are sure to be well satisfied.

- 1 c. dried lentils, rinsed
- 14-oz. pkg. turkey Kielbasa, sliced 1/2-inch thick
- 6 c. beef broth
- 1 c. onion, chopped
- 1 c. celery, chopped
- 1 c. carrots, peeled and chopped
- 1 c. redskin potato, diced
- 2 T. fresh flat-leaf parsley, chopped
- 1/2 t. pepper
- 1/8 t. ground nutmeg

1 Combine all ingredients in a 3-quart slow cooker. Cover and cook on high setting for one hour. Reduce heat to low setting and cook 3 hours. Stir before serving.

Makes about 10 cups

BRUNSWICK STEW

SUE HOGARTH
LANCASTER, CA

When I was young, every November my dad's city friends came for the first day of deer hunting season. They were never successful and came back very hungry! My mom always made big batches of this hearty stew for them outdoors in a Dutch oven on a tripod over an open fire. What a wonderful day of friendship and blessings!

1 Sauté together bacon and onion in a 4-quart Dutch oven until onion is golden, about 5 minutes.

2 Add chicken broth, 2 cups water, celery and salt to Dutch oven. Bring to a boil; reduce heat and simmer, covered, 45 minutes or just until chicken is tender. Skim fat.

3 Remove bones from chicken; discard and return meat to pot. Add tomatoes, potatoes, okra and lima beans. Bring to a boil; reduce heat and simmer, covered, 15 minutes or until potatoes are tender. Add corn and Worcestershire sauce; heat to boiling. Mix flour with remaining water in a small bowl; stir into broth. Cook and stir until thickened.

Makes 6 servings

2 slices bacon
1 c. onion, chopped
3 lbs. chicken
2 10-3/4 oz. cans chicken broth
2-1/4 c. water, divided
1/3 c. celery, chopped
2 t. salt
16-oz. can stewed tomatoes
2 c. potatoes, peeled and diced
10-oz. pkg. frozen okra, thawed
10-oz. pkg. frozen baby lima beans, thawed
12-oz. can corn, drained
1 T. Worcestershire sauce
3 T. all-purpose flour

CHEESY ROTINI & BROCCOLI

MARIAN BUCKLEY
FONTANA, CA

Replace the broccoli with asparagus tips for variety.

1-1/2 c. rotini pasta, uncooked
2 carrots, peeled and sliced
1 c. broccoli flowerets
10-3/4 oz. can Cheddar cheese soup
1/2 c. milk
1/2 c. shredded Cheddar cheese
1 T. mustard

1 Cook pasta according to package directions. Add carrots and broccoli during last 5 minutes of cooking time; drain and return to pot. Pour soup, milk, cheese and mustard into pasta mixture; heat through.

Serves 4

SIDEKICK VEGGIES

CHARLENE MCCAIN
BAKERSFIELD, CA

This is the perfect side dish for any dinner or barbecue. It also works very well as the filling for a chicken pot pie. It's best served hot.

6 red potatoes, diced
3 carrots, peeled and sliced
1 onion, diced
3 stalks celery, chopped
4 T. butter, cubed
salt and pepper to taste

1 Combine vegetables in a microwave-safe dish. Add enough water to nearly cover vegetables; cover with a lid. Microwave on high for 25 minutes, or until vegetables are fork-tender. Drain; transfer vegetables to an ungreased 13"x9" baking pan. Lightly sprinkle with salt and pepper; dot with butter. Place pan under the broiler for about 10 minutes, until potatoes begin to turn golden, being careful not to burn. Stir just before serving; add more salt and pepper as desired.

Makes 6 to 8 servings

CHICKEN TORTILLA SOUP

LYNNETTE ZEIGLER
SOUTH LAKE TAHOE, CA

This is a great make-ahead soup, but don't ladle it over the tortilla chips until just before serving.

1 Sauté onion, pepper, garlic and chicken in oil in a Dutch oven 7 to 8 minutes; remove chicken. Pour in broth; bring to a simmer. Add corn and cumin; cook 10 minutes.

2 Shred chicken; stir into soup. Place some chips in each bowl; ladle soup over chips. Sprinkle with cheese; stir. Top with sour cream and cilantro, if desired.

Serves 6 to 8

1 c. red onion, chopped

1 red pepper, chopped

2 cloves garlic, minced

2 boneless, skinless chicken breasts

1 T. oil

7 c. chicken broth

9-oz. pkg. frozen corn, thawed

1 t. ground cumin

2 c. tortilla chips, lightly crushed

1 c. shredded Cheddar cheese

Optional: sour cream, chopped fresh cilantro

ROASTED ASPARAGUS WITH FETA

DENISE NEAL
YORBA LINDA, CA

Sometimes I add freshly chopped basil, garlic and bowtie pasta... delicious any way you make it!

1 Arrange asparagus spears in a lightly greased 2-quart casserole dish; sprinkle with olive oil and add salt to taste. Bake at 400 degrees for 15 to 20 minutes, until tender; let cool. Chop into 2-inch pieces and toss with tomatoes and feta cheese.

Serves 4

1 bunch asparagus, trimmed

1 to 2 t. olive oil

coarse salt to taste

2 tomatoes, chopped

8-oz. pkg. crumbled feta cheese

TAKE-IT-EASY TORTELLINI SOUP

DANIELLE DORWARD
SAN DIEGO, CA

This easy, creamy soup is so versatile and filling. My five-year-old daughter Annalise always asks for a second helping. Homemade sauce adds great flavor, but your favorite jar sauce works, too!

1/2 lb. ground beef
1/2 onion, diced
3 cloves garlic, minced
1 to 2 T. olive oil
1 carrot, peeled and minced
5 c. spaghetti sauce
8-oz. pkg. cream cheese, room temperature and cubed
4 c. chicken broth
1-1/2 c. zucchini, shredded
5-oz. pkg. fresh baby spinach
1/2 c. sliced cremini or button mushrooms
19-oz. pkg. refrigerated cheese-filled tortellini, uncooked
pepper to taste
Garnish: shredded Parmesan cheese

1 In a large stockpot over medium heat, brown beef, onion and garlic in olive oil. Drain; add carrot and cook another 2 minutes. Stir in sauce. Use a whisk to stir in cream cheese until smooth. Add broth; bring to a boil. Reduce heat to medium-low; simmer for about 10 minutes, stirring occasionally.

2 Add zucchini, spinach, mushrooms and tortellini. Simmer for 7 to 9 more minutes, just until tortellini is warmed through and tender. Season with pepper. Serve soup topped with Parmesan cheese.

Makes 4 to 6 servings

KITCHEN TIP

Convert your favorite stovetop soup recipe to fix and forget in a slow cooker. Most soups that simmer for 2 hours will be done in 4 to 5 hours on high in a slow cooker.

CREAMY CHICKEN-CHEESE SOUP

DENISE PENDLETON
CHINO HILLS, CA

My kids especially love this soup...mostly because they get to add a spoonful of shredded cheese on top!

1 In a saucepan over medium-low heat, cook onion in butter for 8 to 10 minutes, until tender and golden. Stir in flour. Slowly add milk, broth, sauce and pepper. Cook and stir until thickened and bubbly.

2 Stir in chicken and 1/2 cup cheese. Cook and stir over low heat until cheese melts. Top each bowl with a spoonful of remaining cheese.

Makes 4 servings

1/4 onion, chopped
3 T. butter
1/3 c. all-purpose flour
2 c. milk
10-1/2 oz. can chicken broth
1 t. Worcestershire sauce
1/4 t. pepper
12-1/2 oz. can chunk chicken breast, drained and flaked
1 c. shredded Cheddar cheese, divided

TOMATO-TARRAGON SOUP

REBECCA WOOD
ESCONDIDO, CA

Every year my vegetable garden overflows with vine-ripened tomatoes. This is what I make with them!

1 Peel tomatoes, reserving all the juice; strain seeds from juice. Chop tomatoes and combine with juice; set aside. Melt one tablespoon butter in a large saucepan over medium-low heat. Add shallot; sauté until translucent. Add garlic; sauté for one minute, just until golden. Melt remaining butter with shallot mixture. Stir in flour, salt and pepper; cook and stir until thickened and lightly golden. Stir in tomatoes and juice; add herbs. Increase heat to medium. Bring to a simmer; stir constantly until mixture begins to thicken.

2 Reduce heat to low. Cover and simmer for 15 minutes. Cool slightly; purée soup in a blender until smooth. Return soup to saucepan. Warm through and serve hot, or cover, refrigerate and serve chilled.

Makes 4 servings

2 lbs. tomatoes
2 T. butter, divided
1 shallot, minced
2 cloves garlic, minced
2 T. all-purpose flour
1/4 t. salt
1/2 t. pepper
2 T. fresh tarragon, chopped
1 T. fresh parsley, chopped

CRISPY GOLDEN PARMESAN POTATOES

JO ANN
GOOSEBERRY PATCH

We love potatoes! I'm always tickled to find a tasty new way to fix them. This recipe is scrumptious.

1/4 c. butter, melted and divided
1/2 c. grated Parmesan cheese
1 t. garlic powder
1-3/4 lbs. Yukon gold potatoes, halved lengthwise

1 Spread one tablespoon melted butter in a 13"x9" baking pan; place remaining butter in a small bowl. Mix cheese and garlic powder in a separate small bowl. Dip cut sides of potatoes into butter, then into cheese mixture. Place cut-side down in baking pan. Drizzle with any remaining butter. Bake, uncovered, at 400 degrees for 30 to 35 minutes, until tender.

Makes 6 to 8 servings

SLOW-COOKER CHILE VERDE SOUP

LISA SETT
THOUSAND OAKS, CA

Just the right combination of spices makes this an all-time favorite!

1/2 lb. pork tenderloin, cut into 1/2-inch cubes
1 t. oil
2 c. chicken broth
2 15-oz. cans white beans, drained and rinsed
2 4-oz. cans diced green chiles
1/4 t. ground cumin
1/4 t. dried oregano
salt and pepper to taste
Optional: chopped fresh cilantro

1 Cook pork in oil in a skillet over medium heat for one to 2 minutes, until browned. Place pork in a 4-quart slow cooker. Add remaining ingredients except cilantro; stir well. Cover and cook on low setting for 4 to 6 hours. Sprinkle cilantro over each serving, if desired.

Serves 8

CRONINS' SAGE DRESSING

**PAT MARTIN
RIVERSIDE, CA**

Our family has been enjoying this holiday dressing since the 50s...it's been my job to make it since 1972. I always double the recipe to make sure we have plenty of leftovers to share. I've even made it vegan-friendly for our son by substituting vegan butter and vegetable broth and it's still excellent. So simple, yet so good!

1 In a very large bowl, combine bread cubes and parsley; set aside. Dissolve bouillon in boiling water; set aside.

2 Place butter in an 8-cup glass measuring cup. Microwave on high until melted, one to 2 minutes. Add onion, celery, sage, salt and bouillon mixture. Microwave until vegetables are tender, 10 to 12 minutes.

3 Pour over bread cube mixture; mix gently. Spoon into a buttered 13"x9" baking pan. Bake at 350 degrees for 30 to 34 minutes, until heated through and golden on top. May also be used to stuff a large turkey, up to 20 pounds; roast as preferred.

Makes 10 servings

20 c. dry bread cubes
3 T. dried parsley
1 t. chicken bouillon granules
3/4 c. boiling water
1 c. butter, sliced
1-1/2 c. onion, diced
1-1/2 c. celery, diced
1 T. ground sage
2 t. salt

FLORENTINE MEATBALL SOUP

YVONNE VAN BRIMMER
APPLE VALLEY, CA

This is a toss-together soup I came up with for a potluck at church.
It's a breeze to make in a slow cooker.

14-oz. pkg. frozen
  Italian-style meatballs

16-oz. pkg. frozen green
  beans

16-oz. pkg. baby carrots

2 14-1/2 oz. cans sliced
  zucchini with Italian-
  style tomato sauce

2 14-1/2 oz. cans diced
  tomatoes

4 c. fresh baby spinach

1 T. Italian seasoning

1 T. granulated garlic,
  or more to taste

1 yellow onion, chopped

salt and pepper to taste

2 to 3 32-oz. containers
  beef broth

Garnish: grated
  Parmesan cheese

1 To a 6-quart slow cooker, add all ingredients except broth and garnish in the order given; do not drain zucchini or tomatoes. Add enough broth to fill slow cooker 3/4 full. Stir to combine well.

2 Cover and cook on low setting for 8 to 10 hours. Season with more salt and pepper, as desired. Ladle into bowls; sprinkle with Parmesan cheese.

Makes 10 to 12 servings

ICEBOX MASHED POTATOES

PAT MARTIN
RIVERSIDE, CA

These potatoes are delicious with gravy, but really don't need any topping because they are so creamy and good! I've used this recipe for Thanksgiving for over 30 years. It's a wonderful make-ahead dish and travels well too.

1 Cover potatoes with water in a deep stockpot; add bouillon and garlic salt. Bring to a boil over high heat; cook until potatoes are tender, about 20 minutes. Remove from heat; drain into a colander.

2 Return potatoes to the same pot and mash. Add remaining ingredients except butter; mix well. Spoon potatoes into a greased 13"x9" baking pan; dot with butter. Cool slightly; cover with plastic wrap and refrigerate up to 3 days.

3 To serve, let stand at room temperature for 30 minutes. Uncover; bake at 350 degrees for 40 minutes. If top browns too quickly, cover with aluminum foil for the last 10 minutes. May also be reheated in a microwave oven on 80% power for 30 minutes, rotating occasionally.

Makes 10 to 12 servings

5 lbs. baking potatoes, peeled and halved
2 t. chicken bouillon granules
1/2 t. garlic salt
16-oz. container sour cream
8-oz. pkg. cream cheese
2 t. onion powder
2 t. salt
1/4 t. pepper
2 T. butter, sliced

INDIAN CORN STEW

SUSAN JACOBS
VISTA, CA

*My mom used to make this hearty soup whenever our family went
camping, right after we set up camp. Nowadays we like it on a chilly night.
The crusty bread is perfect for dipping in the stew. Leftovers are great
warmed up for lunch the next day.*

1 lb. bacon, cut into
 1-inch pieces
1 onion, chopped
28-oz. can stewed
 tomatoes
29-oz. can tomato sauce
2 15-oz. cans cut green
 beans, drained
2 15-oz. cans corn,
 drained
pepper to taste
2 c. shredded Cheddar
 cheese
Garnish: crusty bread,
 butter
Optional: hot pepper
 sauce to taste

1 In a large saucepan over medium-high heat, cook bacon until crisp; drain most of drippings. Add onion; reduce heat to medium and cook until tender. Add undrained tomatoes, tomato sauce, beans, corn and pepper; heat through.

2 To serve, ladle into 6 soup bowls and top with cheese. Serve with crusty bread, butter and hot sauce, if desired.

Serves 6

LOIS'S BAKED BEANS

SANDY PERRY
BAKERSFIELD, CA

This is an easy recipe from my mother-in-law. Great served hot with a meal or cold with a picnic!

1 Mix together undrained beans and remaining ingredients in a bowl. Transfer to a greased one-quart bean pot or casserole dish. Bake, uncovered, at 350 degrees for one hour, until hot and bubbly.

Makes 4 to 6 servings

32-oz. can pork & beans
1 c. brown sugar, packed
2 T. dry mustard
2 T. smoke-flavored cooking sauce

LUAU BAKED BEANS

SUSAN JACOBS
VISTA, CA

Great for picnics and cookouts! I served this easy dish at the luau we hosted for our daughter when she received her doctorate degree.

1 In a large skillet over medium heat, cook bacon to desired crispness; drain. Add onion; cook with bacon until tender. Stir in remaining ingredients. Reduce heat to low; simmer until warmed through, 10 to 15 minutes.

Serves 15

1 lb. bacon, cut into 1-inch pieces
1/2 onion, chopped
16-oz. bottle barbecue sauce
2 28-oz. cans baked beans, drained
20-oz. can crushed pineapple, drained

MEXICALI RICE

MARIAN BUCKLEY
FONTANA, CA

Serve this with chicken or turkey breasts to make it even heartier!

15-1/4 oz. can corn, drained

15-oz. can black beans, drained and rinsed

4-oz. can diced green chiles

1 onion, chopped

1 red pepper, chopped

2 c. long-cooking rice, uncooked

3-1/2 c. boiling water

1/2 c. frozen orange juice concentrate, thawed

4-1/2 T. lime juice, divided

1-1/2 T. ground cumin

1 T. chili powder

1/3 c. fresh cilantro, chopped

1/2 t. salt

1 Combine corn, black beans, chiles, onion, pepper, rice, water, orange juice, 1/4 cup lime juice, cumin and chili powder in a 3-quart slow cooker.

2 Cover and cook on low setting for 2-1/2 to 3 hours. Stir in remaining lime juice, cilantro and salt; mix well.

Serves 4 to 6

KITCHEN TIP

Leftover green or red pepper and onion can be chopped and kept in a plastic bag in the freezer for up to 2 months to use in other recipes.

MEXICAN CARROTS

JUDY BORECKY
ESCONDIDO, CA

These cool and spicy carrots are something a little different for your taco night dinner.

1 In a saucepan, cover carrots with water. Cook over medium-high heat just until tender; drain. In a serving bowl, combine carrots, jalapeño peppers with juice and remaining ingredients; mix all together. Cover and chill at least 3 hours.

Serves 6 to 8

2 lbs. carrots, peeled
  and sliced on the
  diagonal
4-oz. can diced jalapeño
  peppers
1 onion, thinly sliced
2 T. oil
1 c. white vinegar
salt and pepper to taste

SMOKY SAUSAGE STEW

MARLENE DARNELL
NEWPORT BEACH, CA

Add a little hot pepper sauce if you like.

1 Set aside 1/4 cup beef broth. Combine remaining beef broth, tomatoes, bratwurst, potatoes, onions and carrots in a large stockpot over medium heat.

2 Bring to a boil; reduce heat and simmer for 15 to 20 minutes until vegetables are tender. Combine reserved broth with flour, stirring until smooth; stir into pot until thickened. Add green pepper; simmer 3 minutes.

Serves 6

14-1/2 oz. can beef
  broth, divided
14-1/2 oz. can stewed
  tomatoes
16-oz. pkg. smoked
  bratwurst, sliced
4 new potatoes, cubed
2 onions, coarsely
  chopped
1 c. baby carrots
1/4 c. all-purpose flour
1 green pepper, diced

OH-SO-EASY CORN CHOWDER

SUSAN OWENS
REDLANDS, CA

This satisfying soup goes together in a snap! Garnish individual servings with sour cream and chopped chives, if you like.

2 15-oz. cans new potatoes, drained and diced

2 15-oz. cans creamed corn

15-oz. can corn, drained

16-oz. can chicken, drained

2-oz. jar chopped pimentos, drained

salt and pepper to taste

1 Mix all ingredients in a stockpot over medium heat. Cook until bubbly and heated through.

Serves 6

BONUS IDEA

Have a potluck soup night. Ask friends and neighbors to bring over their favorite soup to share. You provide the bread, crackers and dessert.

PAT'S LENTIL & HAM SOUP

PAT MARTIN
RIVERSIDE, CA

Always the dilemma about the leftover ham bone...what to make, split pea soup or lentil soup? This lentil soup wins my vote, as it is hearty and full of vegetables. The next day it is out-of-this-world good! Hubby hums while he eats it.

1 Heat oil in a Dutch oven over medium heat; add onion, carrots and lentils. Cook until vegetables are softened, about 5 minutes. Stir in broth and seasonings; bring to a boil. Add ham bone and potatoes; reduce heat to medium-low.

2 Simmer, covered, until thickened and lentils are tender, about one hour, stirring occasionally. Discard ham bone and bay leaf. Ladle 1/4 to 1/2 of soup into a blender; cover and process carefully until smooth.

3 Return puréed soup to pot. May also use an immersion blender to purée some of soup right in the pot, while leaving it chunky but thick. Stir in ham. Cover and simmer about 5 minutes, until heated through. Season with salt and pepper.

Makes 8 servings

2 T. olive oil

1 onion, chopped

2 carrots, peeled and diced

2 c. dried brown lentils

8 c. low-sodium chicken broth

1 t. garlic powder or garlic salt

1/2 t. dried thyme

1/4 t. red pepper flakes

1 bay leaf

1 meaty ham bone

2 russet potatoes, peeled and diced

2 c. cooked ham, chopped

salt and pepper to taste

TONY'S PEASANT SOUP

**LINDA CUELLAR
RIVERSIDE, CA**

My husband isn't a big fan of soup, but he does love this one! Serve with crusty Italian bread.

1 T. olive oil

1 lb. sweet Italian pork sausage links, cut into 1/2-inch slices

1/2 lb. boneless, skinless chicken breast, cut into 1/2-inch cubes

3/4 c. onion, chopped

1/2 t. garlic, minced

14-1/2 oz. can chicken broth

14-1/2 oz. can diced tomatoes with basil, garlic and oregano

15-oz. can cannellini beans, drained

Optional: 1/2 t. red pepper flakes

1 c. fresh basil, chopped

Garnish: grated Parmesan cheese

1 Heat oil in a large heavy saucepan over medium heat. Cook sausage and chicken until no longer pink. Add onion and garlic; cook until soft and translucent. Drain; add broth, undrained tomatoes, beans and red pepper flakes, if using.

2 Bring to a boil. Reduce heat to low; cover and simmer for 15 to 20 minutes. Stir in basil and cook for another 10 minutes. Ladle into bowls and sprinkle with cheese.

Serves 4 to 6

REBECCA'S FIDEO SOUP

REBECCA GONZALEZ
MORENO VALLEY, CA

*I hadn't tried this recipe before my husband & I were married...
now I make it often during the winter and whenever the kids are
under the weather. It's very simple but very flavorful and filling.*

1 Combine tomatoes, onion and water in a blender;
process until smooth and set aside.

2 Heat oil in a large saucepan over medium-high
heat; add pasta and peppers, if using. Sauté until
pasta turns a deep golden color. Carefully add
tomato mixture, broth and tomato sauce. Reduce
heat to low; cover and simmer until pasta is
cooked through.

Serves 6 to 8

3 roma tomatoes,
  quartered
1/2 onion
2 c. water
2 T. oil
8-oz. pkg. fideo
  vermicelli pasta,
  uncooked
Optional: 1 to 2 dried
  chile de arbol peppers
4 c. chicken broth
8-oz. can tomato sauce

ALL-TIME-FAVORITE RECIPES FROM *California* SOUTHERN CALIFORNIA COOKS **63**

SPECTACULAR CHICKEN SOUP

KATHLEEN STURM
CORONA, CA

I concocted this recipe while babysitting for my five-year-old nephew,
Dustin, who is rather a picky eater. Dustin loved this soup!

1-1/2 c. celery, diced

1-1/2 c. carrot, peeled and diced

1/4 c. oil

2 T. onion powder

2 T. celery leaves, finely chopped

2 c. cooked chicken, diced

2 49-oz. cans chicken broth

1 c. orzo pasta, cooked

1 In a large soup pot over medium heat, sauté celery and carrot in oil. Drain; sprinkle with onion powder. Add celery leaves, chicken and broth; heat through. Spoon cooked pasta into individual soup bowls; ladle hot soup over top.

Serves 6 to 8

TEA ROOM SQUASH SOUP

**CHARMIE FISHER
FONTANA, CA**

*This recipe was given to me many years ago by a friend. It is such a
rich and satisfying soup...perfect on a chilly autumn evening.*

1 Combine squash and onions in a large saucepan;
cover with water. Cook over medium heat until
vegetables are fork-tender. Drain most of the liquid.

2 Working in batches, purée mixture in a food
processor until smooth; transfer to a large saucepan.
Add remaining ingredients. Heat through over
medium-low heat, until cheese is melted. Serve soup
in small bowls.

Makes 8 servings

6 to 8 crookneck yellow
  squash, sliced
2 onions, chopped
1 t. garlic powder
1/2 c. butter
1/4 t. baking soda
16-oz. pkg. pasteurized
  process cheese spread,
  cubed
2 c. half-and-half
salt to taste

PRESENTATION

Not enough soup bowls that match for
your party? Mixing and matching
different styles of dinnerware is always
fun. Stack a variety of bowls in the
center of the table and let each guest
choose the one they want.

CHAPTER FOUR

DRESSED FOR
Dinner

WHETHER YOU PLAN TO

SERVE DINNER CASUAL

CALIFORNIA-STYLE OR

PLAN A MEAL WITH MORE

SOPHISTICATED FARE,

YOU'LL FIND THE PERFECT

RECIPE IN THIS CHAPTER

OF MAIN DISHES FOR ALL

OCCASIONS.

ANGEL HAIR PASTA & VEGGIES

GLORYA HENDRICKSON
HESPERIA, CA

This recipe came about when I decided to add veggies to some pasta and make it a filling, meatless meal. My family loves this dish and we don't even miss the meat!

3 T. olive oil, divided
1 zucchini, chopped
1 yellow squash, chopped
1 green pepper, chopped
1 onion, chopped
2 to 3 cloves garlic, minced
24-oz. jar marinara pasta sauce
16-oz. pkg. angel hair pasta, uncooked
Optional: grated Parmesan or Romano cheese

1 Heat 2 tablespoons oil in a large skillet or Dutch oven over medium heat. Sauté vegetables and garlic until crisp-tender; drain. Stir in pasta sauce. Reduce heat to low. Cover and simmer for about 30 minutes, stirring occasionally, until thickened. Meanwhile, cook pasta according to package directions; drain and toss with remaining oil. Serve vegetable mixture over cooked pasta. Top with grated cheese, if desired.

Makes 6 servings

BAKED VEGGIES & BACON

CHARLENE MCCAIN
BAKERSFIELD, CA

My family requests this delicious side dish whenever we get together. It's wonderful for barbecues and quick dinners, too.

6 to 8 redskin potatoes, cubed
6 carrots, peeled and sliced
2 stalks celery, chopped
1 yellow onion, chopped
1 c. water
salt and pepper to taste
1/4 c. butter, diced
4 slices bacon, crisply cooked and crumbled

1 Combine vegetables in a large microwave-safe dish; add water. Cover dish with plastic wrap. Microwave for 20 minutes, or until vegetables are tender. Drain water; transfer vegetables to an ungreased 3-quart casserole dish. Season with salt and pepper; dot with butter. Top with bacon.

2 Bake, uncovered, at 400 degrees for 15 minutes, or until potatoes begin to turn golden. Do not overbake.

Makes 8 servings

SPANISH-STYLE ROUND STEAK

**GAYNOR SIMMONS
HEMET, CA**

Thirty-five years ago when my children were little, I put this together with what I had in my pantry. They still request it!

1 In a skillet, brown beef in oil. Add onion and garlic; cook and stir until onion is tender. Drain; stir in vegetable juice, broth, water, salt and pepper. Bring to a boil.

2 Cover; reduce heat and simmer 30 minutes. Add rice, peas and pimentos. Return to a boil. Cover; reduce heat and simmer an additional 20 minutes, or until rice is tender.

Serves 6 to 8

1-1/2 lbs. beef round steak or stew beef, cubed

2 T. olive oil

1/2 c. onion, chopped

1 clove garlic, minced

12-oz. can cocktail vegetable juice

10-1/2 oz. can beef broth

1-1/2 c. water

1-1/2 t. salt

1/4 t. pepper

1-1/2 c. long-cooking rice, uncooked

10-oz. pkg. frozen peas

1/4 c. chopped pimentos

BBQ PORK RIBS

DIANE GREGORI
RIVERSIDE, CA

A big platter of corn on the cob is the perfect partner for these juicy ribs.

3 qts. water
4 lbs. pork ribs, cut into
  serving-size portions
1 onion, quartered
2 t. salt
1/4 t. pepper

1 Bring water to a boil in a large stockpot. Add ribs, onion, salt and pepper. Reduce heat; cover and simmer for 1-1/2 hours.

2 Remove ribs from pot; drain. Grill ribs for 10 minutes on each side, brushing frequently with BBQ Sauce, until tender.

Serves 4 to 6

BBQ SAUCE:
1/2 c. vinegar
1 T. lemon juice
1/2 c. chili sauce
1/4 c. Worcestershire
  sauce
2 T. onion, chopped
1/2 c. brown sugar,
  packed
1/2 t. dry mustard
1/8 t. garlic powder
1/8 t. cayenne pepper

1 Combine all ingredients in a small saucepan. Simmer over low heat for one hour, stirring frequently.

OUSAND OAKS DIEGO ... VINE ... CAJON GARDE
SANTA ... WEST ... ANHEIM

BETTER-THAN-EVER BEEF STROGANOFF

**TRISHA MACQUEEN
BAKERSFIELD, CA**

You only need one skillet to whip up this favorite.

1 Dredge steak in flour; sprinkle with pepper. Melt butter in a skillet over medium heat. Add steak and brown on both sides. Add mushrooms, onion and garlic; sauté until tender. Stir in broth and reduce heat; cover and simmer one hour.

2 Blend in soup and sour cream; simmer 5 more minutes. Do not boil. Spoon over warm noodles to serve.

Serves 4

1-1/2 lbs. beef round steak, sliced
1/4 c. all-purpose flour
pepper to taste
1/2 c. butter
4-oz. can sliced mushrooms, drained
1/2 c. onion, chopped
1 clove garlic, minced
10-1/2 oz. can beef broth
10-3/4 oz. can cream of mushroom soup
1 c. sour cream
6-oz. pkg. medium egg noodles, cooked

SAUCY PORK CHOPS

**CINDY MCCORMICK
BAKERSFIELD, CA**

This saucy bake works well with chicken too!

1 Mix soup, catsup and Worcestershire sauce together; set aside. Arrange pork chops in an ungreased 13"x9" baking pan; pour soup mixture over the top. Cover and bake for one hour at 350 degrees. Serve each pork chop on a serving of rice; spoon remaining sauce on top.

Makes 4 to 6 servings

2 10-3/4 oz. cans cream of chicken soup
1/2 c. catsup
2 T. Worcestershire sauce
4 to 6 pork chops
2-1/2 c. cooked rice

CHEESE-STUFFED PASTA SHELLS

KATHLEEN STURM
CORONA, CA

Filled with three kinds of cheese, these saucy shells are perfect for a special dinner...always welcome at potlucks too.

12-oz. pkg. jumbo pasta shells, uncooked
32-oz. container ricotta cheese
8-oz. pkg. shredded mozzarella cheese
1 T. fresh Italian parsley, chopped
1/2 c. grated Parmesan cheese
2 eggs, lightly beaten
1/2 t. salt
1/4 t. pepper
1/8 t. nutmeg
3 c. pasta sauce, divided
Garnish: additional mozzarella and Parmesan cheese

1 Cook pasta shells according to package directions; drain. Meanwhile, in a bowl, combine remaining ingredients except pasta sauce and garnish. Spread 1/2 cup pasta sauce in a greased 13"x9" baking pan; set aside.

2 With a spoon, carefully fill each cooked shell with 1-1/2 tablespoons cheese filling. Arrange filled shells in baking pan, making layers of sauce and shells as needed. Pour remaining sauce over and around shells. Sprinkle with additional cheeses to taste. Cover tightly with aluminum foil.

3 Bake at 375 degrees for 35 minutes, or until hot and bubbly. If using frozen shells, add a few minutes to the baking time.

Makes 5 to 6 servings

CHEESEBURGER BAKE

JENNIFER WILLIAMS,
LOS ANGELES, CA

This hearty meal is great after a long day of work and errands...so filling.

1 Unroll crescent roll dough; separate triangles and press into a greased 9" round baking pan, pinching seams closed. Bake at 350 degrees for 10 minutes; set aside. Meanwhile, brown beef in a skillet over medium heat; drain. Add taco seasoning and sauce; heat through. Spoon over crescent rolls and sprinkle cheese on top.

2 Bake, uncovered, for 10 to 15 minutes. Let stand 5 minutes before serving. Garnish with chopped green onions.

Serves 4

8-oz. tube refrigerated crescent rolls
1 lb. ground beef
1-1/4 oz. pkg. taco seasoning mix
15-oz. can tomato sauce
2 c. shredded Cheddar cheese
Garnish: chopped green onions

ROPA VIEJA DE CUBANO

BREN ROGERS
YORBA LINDA, CA

This recipe is a favorite in our house! "Ropa vieja" translates literally to "old clothes," and the children in our family love to ask for old clothes for dinner.

1 Place steak in a slow cooker, trimming to fit if needed. Pour in tomatoes with juice; add remaining ingredients except salsa. Cover and cook on high setting for 3 hours, or on low setting for 6 hours, until steak is fork-tender. Shred steak using 2 forks. Stir in salsa.

2 Cook, leaving lid slightly ajar, on high setting for 30 minutes longer, or until liquid has cooked down. Discard bay leaf before serving.

Serves 8

2-lb. beef flank steak
10-oz. can diced tomatoes with green chiles
1 onion, diced
2 t. chili powder
1-1/2 t. ground cumin
1 t. dried oregano
1 bay leaf
2 c. salsa

CHICKEN & BLACK BEANS

MARISSA GURGANIOUS
MORENO VALLEY, CA

I wanted to share a recipe that my husband and I just love!

4 to 5 boneless, skinless
  chicken breasts
15-oz. can black beans,
  drained and rinsed
15-oz. can corn, drained
16-oz. jar salsa
8-oz. pkg. cream cheese,
  cubed

1 Place chicken in a slow cooker. Add beans and corn; pour salsa over top. Cover and cook on high setting for 4 hours. Add cream cheese. Cover and cook on high for 30 minutes longer, or until cream cheese melts. Stir sauce before serving.

Serves 4 to 5

ROSEMARY PORK & MUSHROOMS

VICKIE
GOOSEBERRY PATCH

This simple dish is delicious with ordinary button mushrooms, but for a special dinner I'll use a combination of wild mushrooms...their earthy flavor goes so well with fresh rosemary.

1 lb. pork tenderloin, cut
  into 8 slices
1 T. butter
1 c. sliced mushrooms
2 T. onion, finely
  chopped
1 clove garlic, minced
1 t. fresh rosemary,
  chopped
1/4 t. celery salt
1 T. sherry or apple
  juice

1 Flatten each pork slice to one-inch thick; set aside. Melt butter in a large skillet over medium-high heat. Cook pork slices just until golden, about one minute per side. Remove pork slices to a plate, reserving drippings in skillet. Add remaining ingredients except sherry or apple juice to skillet. Reduce heat to low; cook for 2 minutes, stirring frequently. Stir in sherry or juice. Return pork slices to skillet; spoon mushroom mixture over top. Cover and simmer for 3 to 4 minutes, until pork juices run clear. Serve pork slices topped with mushroom mixture.

Makes 4 servings, 2 slices each

CHICKEN & SAUSAGE SKILLETINI

ELIZABETH CISNEROS
CHINO HILLS, CA

My husband loves any kind of sausage, and combining it with chicken breasts is a great way to serve it without eating too much!

1 Heat oil in a large skillet over medium heat. Add chicken, sausage, onion and garlic; cook until juices run clear when chicken is pierced.

2 Add tomatoes, red pepper, brown sugar, basil, oregano, salt and pepper; simmer 5 minutes. Add cooked pasta and simmer an additional 5 minutes. Garnish with oregano, if desired.

Serves 8

2 T. olive oil

2 boneless, skinless chicken breasts, cubed

1/2 lb. spicy lean ground pork sausage

1 red onion, thinly sliced

2 cloves garlic, minced

14-1/2 oz. can diced tomatoes

1 red pepper, sliced

1 T. brown sugar, packed

1 t. dried basil

1/2 t. dried oregano

1/8 t. pepper

10-oz. pkg. whole-wheat linguine pasta, cooked

Optional: fresh oregano leaves

CHICKEN CACCIATORE

**JENNIFER MINEKHEIM
GARDEN GROVE, CA**

This is a favorite dish for everyone at our house, so I am thankful it is so easy to make!

1 lb. chicken breasts,
  cubed
2 T. oil
28-oz. jar spaghetti
  sauce
14-1/2 oz. can diced
  tomatoes
1 green pepper, chopped
1 onion, chopped
2 cloves garlic, minced
1 t. Italian seasoning
salt and pepper to taste

1 Brown chicken in oil in a large skillet over medium heat. Add spaghetti sauce and stir in remaining ingredients. Simmer until vegetables are tender.

Serves 2 to 4

STOVETOP TUNA CASSEROLE

**SONYA LABBE
LOS ANGELES, CA**

We like tuna casserole, but there are days that I just don't want to use the oven. This casserole is very tasty and is a breeze to make.

8-oz. pkg. elbow
  macaroni, uncooked
6-1/2 oz. container semi-
  soft light garlic &
  herb cheese
1/2 c. milk, divided
2 12-1/4 oz. cans solid
  white tuna in water,
  drained and broken up
2 t. dill weed

1 Cook macaroni according to package directions. Drain; return macaroni to pan. Add cheese and 1/4 cup milk to macaroni. Cook and stir over medium heat until cheese is melted and macaroni is coated, adding remaining milk as needed for a creamy consistency. Gently fold in tuna and dill; heat through.

Makes 4 servings

CHICKEN CHILAQUILES

SHARON GUTIERREZ
ESCONDIDO, CA

I like to figure out shortcuts to make recipes quick & easy. I combined a few different recipes to make this extremely yummy dinner. Try it...I think you'll agree!

1 Heat oil in a skillet over medium heat, until hot. Cook tortilla strips, a few at a time, just until crispy. Drain tortilla strips on paper towels; sprinkle with salt, if desired. Mix cheeses in a bowl; set aside.

2 Spray a 13"x9" baking pan with non-stick vegetable spray. Layer half of the tortilla strips in pan; top with chicken, one cup sauce and one cup cheese mixture. Press layers gently down into pan. Repeat layering with remaining tortilla strips, sauce and cheese. Bake, uncovered, at 350 degrees for about 30 minutes, or until cheese is melted and golden.

Makes 6 to 8 servings

1/2 c. oil

10 corn tortillas, cut into 1/2-inch strips

Optional: salt to taste

1 c. shredded mozzarella cheese

1 c. shredded Cheddar cheese

2 c. cooked chicken, shredded

28-oz. can mild chile verde sauce, divided

CHICKEN MOLE VERDE

SUSANA RODRIGUEZ
RIALTO, CA

*This recipe reminds me of my grandmother, who has long since passed.
She was a wonderful cook and this was one of her favorite recipes.*

3-1/2 lbs. chicken, cut up
1/2 onion
3 cloves garlic, divided
1 T. chicken soup base
1/4 t. salt
6 green tomatoes
1/2 green jalapeño pepper, seeds removed if desired
1/2 c. shelled pumpkin seeds
1/4 c. fresh cilantro, chopped
6 c. cooked Mexican rice

1 Place chicken in a stockpot; cover with water. Add onion, 2 cloves garlic, soup base and salt. Cook over medium-low heat until tender, 45 minutes to one hour. Drain, reserving one cup broth; return chicken to pot.

2 Meanwhile, in a saucepan, cover tomatoes, jalapeño and remaining garlic clove with water. Cook over medium-high heat for 15 to 25 minutes, until tomatoes are soft and opaque green; drain.

3 In a dry skillet over medium-high heat, toast pumpkin seeds until lightly golden, stirring often. Transfer tomato mixture, reserved broth, pumpkin seeds and cilantro into a blender. Process until smooth; add salt. Spoon tomato mixture over chicken. Cover; simmer over low heat until warmed through. Serve with favorite Mexican rice.

Makes 6 servings

CHICKEN OLÉ CASSEROLE

JUDY ADAMS
GARDEN GROVE, CA

Served with a side of sweet corn cake or cheesy refried beans, here's a meal everyone will love...and it's simple to make!

1 Spray a 13"x9" baking pan with non-stick vegetable spray; layer with half the tortilla strips and half the chicken. Set aside.

2 Combine soup, milk, onion, chiles and salsa together; mix well. Spread over the chicken; layer with remaining tortilla strips and chicken. Sprinkle with cheese; bake for 1-1/2 hours at 300 degrees.

Makes 8 servings

10 corn tortillas, sliced into strips and divided

8-oz. pkg. boneless, skinless chicken breasts, cooked

2 10-3/4 oz. cans cream of chicken soup

1 c. milk

1 onion, chopped

7-oz. can chopped green chiles, drained

7-oz. jar salsa

2 c. shredded Cheddar cheese

FUN FACT

The dark meat of the chicken has a few more calories than the white meat but it contains more iron, zinc, riboflavin, thiamine, and vitamins B6 and B12. Whatever you choose, it has less fat than most cuts of red meat.

COUNTRY CAPTAIN

MARLENE DARNELL
NEWPORT BEACH, CA

*We discovered this curry-flavored dish with the unusual name
on a trip to southern Georgia.*

2 T. olive oil

3-lb. chicken, quartered
and skin removed

2 cloves garlic, minced

1 onion, chopped

1 green pepper, chopped

1/2 c. celery, chopped

2 t. curry powder

1/3 c. currants or raisins

14-1/2 oz. can whole
tomatoes, chopped

1 t. sugar

salt and pepper to taste

hot cooked rice

Garnish: 1/4 c. slivered
almonds

1 Heat oil in a skillet over medium heat. Sauté chicken just until golden; place in a 4 to 5-quart slow cooker and set aside. Add garlic, onion, green pepper, celery and curry powder to skillet; sauté briefly.

2 Remove from heat; stir in remaining ingredients except rice and almonds. Pour over chicken. Cover and cook on low setting for 6 hours, until chicken is no longer pink. Serve over cooked rice; garnish with almonds.

Serves 4

All-Day Apple Butter, p. 8

Whether you are looking for a quick-to-make breakfast dish, no-fuss party fare, satisfying soups & sandwiches, main dishes to fill them up, or a sweet little something to savor at the end of the meal, you'll love these recipes from the amazing cooks in beautiful Southern California.

BBQ Pork Ribs, p. 70

Bratwurst & Potato Salad, p. 27

Cheese-Stuffed Pasta Shells, p. 72

Cheeseburger Bake, p. 73

Hashbrown Quiche, p. 16

Pretzel Twists, p. 120

Raspberry Upside-Down Cake, p. 147

Seaside Salmon Buns, p. 31

Slow-Cooker Chile
Verde Soup, p. 52

Spanish-Style Round Steak, p. 69

Sweet Raspberry-Oat
Bars, p. 141

Lighter-Than-Air Potato Rolls, p. 19

The Best Blondies, p. 137

Tomato-Basil
Couscous Salad, p. 32

Chicken Taco Salad, p. 41

Collins' Best Lentil Soup, p. 46

Chicken Tortilla Soup, p. 49

Cranberry Slush, p. 121

Deep-Dish Sausage
Pizza, p. 43

Creamy Basil Salad Dressing, p. 40

Tangy Deviled Eggs, p. 124

Florentine Meatball Soup. p. 54

Grandma & Katie's
Frozen Dessert, p. 137

Pea Salad, p. 28

Scrambled Egg in a Cup, p. 13

Tomato-Tarragon Soup, p. 51

CUBAN BREADED PAN-FRIED STEAKS

PATRICIA AGUERO
BAKERSFIELD, CA

My grandkids love these tasty little steaks! This recipe has been handed down for generations, starting with my own grandmother. I have been making this family favorite for many years.

1 Season steaks on both sides with herbs, salt and pepper; set aside. Beat eggs and milk together in a pie plate; spread bread crumbs onto a large plate. Dip each steak into egg mixture; immediately place in bread crumbs and coat generously on both sides. Set aside steaks on a plate.

2 In a large non-stick skillet, heat oil over medium-high heat. Add steaks; cook until golden on both sides. Turn steaks only once, to prevent coating from falling off.

Makes 4 servings

4 thin sandwich or milanesa-style beef steaks
1 T. dried oregano
1 T. onion powder
1 T. garlic powder
salt and pepper to taste
2 eggs, beaten
1/2 c. milk
2 c. dry bread crumbs
1/2 c. olive oil

CHILI VERDE PORK

CHARLENE MCCAIN
BAKERSFIELD, CA

We love slow-cooked pork with green chiles in our tacos and burritos! The kids just fill a cold flour tortilla and off they run. I like mine tostada style, layering a fried tortilla with warmed refried beans, chili verde and tomato, lettuce, olives and sour cream on top. This makes a lot, but leftovers can be frozen for up to two months.

1 Coat pork cubes with flour; shake off excess. Heat oil in a deep skillet over medium-high heat. Brown pork cubes on all sides; drain. Add remaining ingredients. Reduce heat to low; cover and simmer about 30 minutes.

2 Transfer mixture to a slow cooker. Cover and cook on low setting for 6 to 8 hours, until pork is very tender. Serve as desired.

Serves 6 to 8

2-1/2 to 3-lb. boneless pork roast, cut into large cubes
1/2 c. all-purpose flour
1/4 c. oil
1 onion, diced
7-oz. can chopped green chiles
14-1/2 oz. can chicken broth

CHILE RELLENO CASSEROLE

GEORGIA MALLORY
ANAHEIM, CA

*This is a tasty breakfast, brunch or anytime casserole...yummy served
with sour cream, salsa and lots of fresh melon!*

7-oz. can whole green
chiles, drained

16-oz. pkg. shredded
Monterey Jack cheese,
divided

16-oz. pkg. shredded
Cheddar cheese,
divided

7-oz. can chopped green
chiles

salt and pepper to taste

6 eggs, beaten

13-oz. can evaporated
milk

Optional: salsa and sour
cream

1 Slit whole chiles and remove seeds; rinse and
dry. Lay whole chiles, skin-side down, in a lightly
greased 13"x9" baking pan; sprinkle with half of
each cheese. Top with chopped chiles, remaining
cheese, salt and pepper. In a bowl, combine eggs
and milk; pour over top.

2 Bake, uncovered, at 350 degrees for 45 minutes.
Serve with salsa or sour cream, if desired.

Serves 8

CALIFORNIA COOL

Fish tacos are everywhere in Southern California.
One chain, called Wahoo's, combines a classic
Mexican fish taco with Brazilian and Asian
flavors. Talk about fusion cuisine!

STUFFED FLANK STEAK

LISA SETT
THOUSAND OAKS, CA

This is one of my best slow-cooker recipes...it's easy, delicious and good enough for company! We grow our own blackberries, so I always have blackberry jam on hand, but grape jam and orange marmalade may also be used.

1 With a sharp knife, score steak lightly on both sides without cutting all the way through. Place a 24-inch length of kitchen twine under steak; set aside. In a bowl, mix together remaining ingredients except oil; spread over steak. Roll up steak; tie with twine. Pour oil into a slow cooker. Add steak; turn to coat on all sides.

2 Spoon Gravy over steak. Cover and cook on low setting for 8 to 10 hours, until tender. Remove steak to a platter. Let stand several minutes; discard twine. Slice steak, using an electric knife, if possible.

Serves 6 to 8

1-1/2 lbs. beef flank steak
1-1/2 c. dry bread crumbs
1/2 c. mushrooms, finely diced
1/4 c. grated Parmesan cheese
1/4 c. beef broth
2 T. butter, melted
2 T. oil

1 Combine gravy mix and water in a small saucepan over medium heat. Bring to a boil, stirring frequently. Reduce heat to low; simmer for one minute. Stir in remaining ingredients.

GRAVY:
.87-oz. pkg. brown gravy mix
1 c. water
1/4 c. blackberry jam
1/4 c. apple juice
Optional: 2 T. green onion, minced

CLASSIC CORNED BEEF & CABBAGE

**HEIDI MCINNISH
CHULA VISTA, CA**

A St. Patrick's Day tradition...but much too delicious to enjoy only once a year!

2 to 3 onions, chopped

1-1/4 lbs. baby carrots

3-lb. corned beef brisket with seasoning packet

1/2 c. malt vinegar

Optional: 1/4 c. Irish stout

1-1/4 lbs. redskin potatoes

1 to 1-1/2 heads cabbage, cut into serving-size wedges

Garnish: coarse-grain mustard, Dijon mustard

1 Place onions, carrots, corned beef, seasoning packet, vinegar and stout, if using, in a large stockpot. Add enough water to just cover beef. Cover and bring to a boil. Reduce heat to medium-low and simmer for 2-1/2 to 3 hours, until beef is tender. Add potatoes and cabbage. Increase heat to high; cover and simmer for 8 to 10 minutes. Reduce heat to medium and simmer an additional 15 minutes, or until potatoes are tender.

2 Remove vegetables to a serving dish; place beef on a cutting board. Let rest 3 minutes; slice against the grain. Serve with vegetables and mustards.

Serves 6 to 8

BASIL & TOMATO HALIBUT

DEBRA VAN ZANT
STEVENSON RANCH, CA

Slices of garden-fresh tomatoes and a sprinkle of freshly chopped basil taste amazing spooned over servings of fish.

1 In a skillet over medium heat, sauté onion and garlic in oil and butter for 3 minutes. Stir in tomatoes, broth and seasonings. Add fish to skillet.

2 Cook, covered, over medium heat until fish flakes easily, about 8 minutes. Remove fish from sauce and lay on a bed of rice. Add basil to sauce; stir and spoon over fish and rice.

Makes 6 servings

1 onion, sliced
4 cloves garlic, minced
1 T. olive oil
1 t. butter
8 roma tomatoes, diced
14-1/2 oz. can chicken broth
1 t. seafood seasoning
1/4 t. pepper
2 lbs. halibut fillets
cooked rice
fresh basil to taste, chopped

KITCHEN TIP

A flexible plastic cutting mat makes speedy work of slicing & dicing. Keep two mats on hand for chopping meat and veggies separately.

ON-THE-RUN CHICKEN POT PIE

**CHARLENE MCCAIN
BAKERSFIELD, CA**

*A terrific recipe for those nights when you want a nutritious, homestyle
meal for your family but don't have a lot of time.*

2 potatoes, peeled and
  diced
2 carrots, peeled and
  chopped
1 onion, diced
2 stalks celery, chopped
1 c. water, divided
10-3/4 oz. can cream of
  chicken soup
1/2 c. milk
1 to 1-1/2 c. cooked
  chicken, diced
salt and pepper to taste
1/2 c. frozen peas
9-inch pie crust, cut into
  1-inch wide strips
1 egg, beaten

1 Place potatoes, carrots, onion, celery and
1/2 cup water in a microwave-safe bowl. Cover and
microwave on high for 15 minutes. Meanwhile, heat
soup with milk and remaining water in a saucepan
over medium heat; stir in chicken, salt and pepper.

2 When vegetables are done, drain and place in an
ungreased 2-quart casserole dish. Add peas; spoon
chicken mixture into dish. Arrange pie crust strips
on top lattice-style; brush with egg. Bake at
425 degrees for 15 to 20 minutes, until crust is
golden and mixture is hot and bubbly.

Serves 4

CHICKEN WITH PEPPERS

JENNIFER MINEKHEIM
GARDEN GROVE, CA

This is my go-to recipe for a super quick meal!

1 Brown chicken in oil in a large skillet over medium heat. Add spaghetti sauce and stir in remaining ingredients. Simmer until vegetables are tender and chickenis cooked.

Makes 4 servings

1 lb. boneless, skinless chicken breasts, cubed
1 T. oil
14-1/2 oz. jar spaghetti sauce
14-1/2 oz. can diced tomatoes
1/2 green pepper, chopped
1/2 onion, chopped
2 cloves garlic, minced
1 t. dried Italian spices
1/2 t. pepper

STEWED CHICKEN VERDE

ROBIN ACASIO
CHULA VISTA, CA

This chicken is so tender and juicy...the leftovers make yummy quesadillas too. I love to use my slow cooker and I'm always thinking up new ideas to try. This recipe was a hit with my family.

1 Sprinkle chicken all over with poultry seasoning. Place onion slices and cilantro inside chicken. Place chicken in an oval slow cooker; top with soup and chiles. Cover and cook on low setting for 7 to 8 hours. Serve with cooked rice.

Serves 4 to 6

3 to 3-1/2 lb. whole chicken
1 T. poultry seasoning
1/4 onion, sliced
several sprigs fresh cilantro
10-3/4 oz. can cream of chicken soup
4-oz. can chopped green chiles
cooked rice

DELICIOUS CREAMED TURKEY

or chicken

NANCY WEIFORD
BUENA PARK, CA

The day after Thanksgiving, when my family still wants turkey, but with a new twist, I serve this casserole with a carrot & pineapple-orange gelatin salad...it's always a hit!

3 c. cooked turkey, diced
1/2 c. celery, diced
1/4 c. onion, diced
1 c. peas
1 c. corn
1/2 c. mushrooms, chopped
1/2 c. slivered almonds
1 t. dill weed
1 t. dried thyme
1 t. dried parsley
1 t. dried basil
1/2 t. salt
1/2 t. pepper
2 c. whipping cream
1/2 c. water, ~~divided~~
1 c. shredded Cheddar cheese
Optional: 1 to 4 t. cornstarch
6 English muffins, split and toasted, or 6 puff pastry shells, baked
Garnish: melted butter
Optional: capers

1 In a large saucepan over low heat, combine turkey, vegetables, mushrooms, almonds and seasonings. Add just enough water to cover ingredients by 1/2 inch. Simmer, watching closely, until vegetables are tender and most of water is evaporated.

2 Add cream and 1/2 cup water. Continue to simmer, stirring constantly. Gently stir in cheese. Add cornstarch, one teaspoon at a time, if needed to thicken to desired consistency. Simmer over medium heat for 15 minutes. Serve over English muffin halves or puff pastry shells brushed with butter. Garnish with capers, if desired.

Serves 6

DELICIOUS OVEN BAR-B-QUE RIBS

NANCY HANSON
MURRIETA, CA

I have been making these wonderful ribs for over 35 years now...they never disappoint! They are not only delicious but oh-so easy to prepare. Enjoy!

1 Place ribs in a Dutch oven; cover with water. Bring to a boil over high heat; reduce heat to medium-low. Simmer until ribs are nearly tender, about one hour. Drain ribs and place in a shallow baking pan; discard cooking liquid. To a saucepan over medium heat, add remaining ingredients except onion and lemon. Bring to a boil; cook and stir for 5 minutes.

2 Stir in onion and lemon. Cool; spoon over ribs. Cover and refrigerate up to 24 hours. Bake, uncovered, at 350 degrees for 45 minutes, basting often with pan juices.

Makes 4 servings

4 lbs. pork spareribs or country-style ribs
1 c. catsup
1 c. water
1/3 c. vinegar
1/3 c. brown sugar, packed
3 T. Worcestershire sauce
1 t. dry mustard
1 t. paprika
1 t. salt
1/2 t. chili powder
1 onion, thinly sliced
1/2 lemon, thinly sliced

INSIDE-OUT STUFFED PEPPER

CHARLENE MCCAIN
BAKERSFIELD, CA

A quick and tasty dish for those nights when you get home late and everybody's hungry...super-simple to toss together!

1 green pepper, top
  removed
1 lb. ground beef
1 onion, chopped
1-1/2 c. cooked rice
8-oz. can tomato sauce
salt and pepper to taste

1 Bring a saucepan of salted water to a boil. Add green pepper and cook for 8 to 10 minutes, until tender. Drain; cool slightly and chop pepper. Meanwhile, cook beef and onion in a skillet over medium heat, stirring often, until beef is browned and onion is translucent. Drain; add green pepper and cooked rice to skillet. Pour tomato sauce over beef mixture; stir and heat through. Season with salt and pepper to taste.

Serves 4

SPANISH RICE & BEEF

SUE HOGARTH
LANCASTER, CA

This recipe is perfect when you need to get dinner on the table in a hurry, after working all day and shuttling the kids to their after-school events.

1 lb. ground beef
14-1/2 oz. can stewed
  tomatoes
10-oz. pkg. frozen corn
  or mixed vegetables
1 c. water
1/2 t. dried oregano
1/2 t. chili powder
1/4 t. garlic powder
1/2 t. salt
1/8 t. pepper
1-1/2 c. instant rice,
  uncooked

1 Brown beef in a large skillet over medium heat; drain. Add undrained tomatoes, frozen corn or vegetables, water and seasonings. Bring to a boil; boil about 2 minutes, or until vegetables are tender.

2 Stir in uncooked rice. Cover; remove from heat and let stand about 5 minutes. Fluff rice with a fork before serving.

Makes 4 to 6 servings

LINGUINE & CLAMS

ELIZABETH CISNEROS
EASTVALE, CA

A classic Italian restaurant favorite to savor at home.

1 Cook pasta according to package directions, just until tender; drain. Meanwhile, melt butter with olive oil in a large skillet over medium heat. Add garlic; sauté until tender. Stir in wine or broth and reserved clam liquid; simmer for 10 minutes. Stir in clams and parsley; simmer for 5 more minutes. Toss pasta with sauce; garnish with a sprinkle of pepper.

Serves 4

16-oz. pkg. linguine pasta, uncooked
1/4 c. butter
1/4 c. olive oil
4 cloves garlic, minced
1 c. white wine or clam broth
10-oz. can whole baby clams, drained and liquid reserved
2 T. fresh parsley, minced
Garnish: cracked pepper

TAMALE POT PIE

MARIAN BUCKLEY
FONTANA, CA

Not your "usual" pot pie filling...this will be a hit!1 lb. ground beef

1 Cook ground beef in a large skillet over medium heat until browned; drain. Stir in corn, tomatoes with juice, olives, 2 tablespoons baking mix, chili powder, cumin and salt. Bring to a boil; boil, stirring frequently, one minute. Keep warm over low heat.

2 Stir together remaining baking mix and remaining ingredients until blended. Pour beef mixture into an ungreased 9"x9" baking pan. Spread cornmeal mixture over beef mixture. Bake, uncovered, at 400 degrees for 20 to 30 minutes, until golden.

Serves 6

1 lb. ground beef
2 c. frozen corn, thawed
14-1/2 oz. can diced tomatoes
2-1/4 oz. can sliced black olives, drained
1 c. plus 2 T. biscuit baking mix, divided
1 T. chili powder
2 t. ground cumin
1/2 t. salt
1/2 c. cornmeal
1/2 c. milk
2 T. chopped green chiles
1 egg, beaten

MILD CHILI VERDE

ALTA PADILLA
RIVERSIDE, CA

My husband and I are empty nesters now. But if I mention I'm going to put this into my slow cooker, my kids all come home to eat. I even made this dish for 250 guests at a 25th wedding anniversary dinner! Serve with Mexican rice and refried beans.

4 lbs. boneless pork country ribs, cut into 1-inch cubes

garlic salt to taste

2 T. oil

2 onions, chopped

2 7-oz. cans diced green chiles

14-1/2 oz. can diced tomatoes

24-oz. can thick & chunky salsa verde

1 c. water

2 t. chicken bouillon granules

1/2 t. ground cumin

flour tortillas, warmed

1 Season pork with garlic salt. Heat oil in a large skillet over medium-high heat. Working in batches, brown pork on all sides; remove pork to a slow cooker as it is browned. Drain skillet, reserving one tablespoon oil in skillet. Add onions and sauté until translucent, scraping to get up all of the browned bits in the skillet. Add onions, undrained chiles and tomatoes to slow cooker; stir in salsa, water, bouillon and cumin.

2 Cover and cook on low setting for 6 to 8 hours, or on high setting for 3 hours, until pork is very tender. To serve, shred pork; spoon into warmed tortillas.

Makes 8 to 10 servings

MOM'S SPAGHETTI SAUCE

SUSAN MYRICK
SAN DIEGO, CA

When I was growing up in Michigan, my mom made this on cold winter days.

1 In a skillet over medium heat, brown beef with onion and garlic; drain. Stir in spaghetti sauce, tomatoes with juice, tomato paste and seasonings.

2 Cover and simmer over low to medium-low heat, stirring often, for 3 to 4 hours. Discard bay leaves before serving.

Makes 4 to 6 servings

1 lb. ground beef
1 onion, chopped
2 to 3 cloves garlic, chopped
26-oz. jar spaghetti sauce
28-oz. can crushed tomatoes
6-oz. can tomato paste
celery salt, salt and pepper to taste
1 to 2 bay leaves

VEGETARIAN MEXICAN PIE

SONYA LABBE
WEST HOLLYWOOD, CA

When we moved to Los Angeles, I started searching for Mexican dishes that my family would love. This recipe is one of them. It's easy to make, yet so much better than any fast food.

1 Layer 4 of the tortillas in a lightly greased 8"x8" baking pan, overlapping slightly. Top tortillas with 1/2 cup black beans, 1/2 cup kidney beans, 1/4 cup chiles, 1/2 cup salsa, 1/3 cup yogurt and 1/3 cup cheese. Add 4 more tortillas; repeat layering.

2 Top with remaining tortillas, salsa, sour cream and cheese. Bake, uncovered, at 375 degrees, until bubbly and golden, 30 to 40 minutes.

Makes 6 servings

12 6-inch corn tortillas
1 c. black beans, drained and rinsed
1 c. red kidney beans, drained and rinsed
4-oz. can chopped green chiles
1-1/2 c. green or red salsa
1 c. sour cream
1 c. shredded Monterey Jack cheese

MOONCHA'S CHICKEN CHOW MEIN

SUSAN JACOBS
VISTA, CA

The original recipe came from my Korean aunt in 1967, and I later adapted it to fit my family's tastes. Any leftovers are great for lunch the next day, but a warning...I've found this recipe doesn't go as far with teenagers in the house as it once did with small kids!

3-1/2 lbs. chicken

3 c. long-cooking rice, uncooked

1-1/2 c. celery, sliced

1 c. carrots, peeled and chopped

1 c. onion, chopped

1/4 to 1/2 c. soy sauce

pepper to taste

Optional: 15-oz. can bean sprouts, drained

Garnish: additional soy sauce

1 In a large stockpot, cover chicken with water. Simmer over medium-low heat for about one hour, until chicken is very tender. Remove chicken from stockpot, reserving broth. Let chicken cool. Stir rice into broth in stockpot; simmer for about 10 minutes.

2 Add celery, carrots and onion to stockpot. Continue to simmer for about 10 minutes, until rice and vegetables are tender. Add a little more water if necessary to finish cooking rice; mixture should not be soupy.

3 Shred chicken into bite-size pieces, discarding skin and bones. Stir chicken into rice mixture along with soy sauce, pepper and bean sprouts, if using. Serve in bowls with additional soy sauce on the side.

Makes 10 servings

NANI'S MAC & CHEESE

STARLA SMITH
MANHATTAN BEACH, CA

I was never a fan of homemade mac & cheese until my mother-in-law served this one night. When I tried it, I was hooked! Then I tweaked the recipe to make a savory version...now it's my go-to dish to bring to all the holiday dinners! Either way, it's delicious and satisfying.

1 Cook macaroni according to package instructions; drain. Place macaroni in a 13"x9" baking pan sprayed with non-stick vegetable spray and set aside. Meanwhile, in a large saucepan, combine remaining ingredients except cheese. Bring to a boil over medium heat. Boil for one minute; remove from heat. Add cheese; stir until completely melted. Spoon cheese mixture over macaroni; mix well.

2 Bake, uncovered, at 375 degrees for 20 minutes, or until bubbly and golden.

Serves 10 to 15

16-oz. pkg. elbow or small shell macaroni, uncooked
12-oz. can evaporated milk
1 c. water
2 T. cornstarch
2 T. butter
1/2 t. salt
1/4 t. pepper
16-oz. pkg. shredded sharp Cheddar cheese

Variation:

STARLA'S SAVORY MAC & CHEESE

1 Cook macaroni; place in baking pan as directed above. In a large saucepan, sauté one diced sweet onion in one tablespoon olive oil until tender. Add one to 2 cups diced cooked ham; cook for one to 2 minutes. Add remaining ingredients above, except cheese; bring to a boil. Finish recipe as directed, replacing sharp Cheddar cheese with 1-1/2 cups each shredded Cheddar and Pepper Jack cheese.

ALL-TIME-FAVORITE RECIPES FROM *California* SOUTHERN CALIFORNIA COOKS **101**

QUICK PIZZA MAC

SHEILA MURRAY
LANCASTER, CA

This casserole tastes just like pizza so my family loves it...and I love it because it is so easy!

1-1/2 c. elbow macaroni, cooked
8-oz. jar pizza sauce
8-oz. container cottage cheese
4-oz. pkg. sliced pepperoni, halved
1/2 c. onion, chopped
1/2 t. dried basil
1 T. grated Parmesan cheese

1 In a lightly greased 2-quart casserole dish, combine all ingredients except Parmesan cheese; blend well. Sprinkle Parmesan over top. Cover; bake at 350 degrees for 30 to 35 minutes, or until heated through.

Serves 6

STIR-FRY PORK & NOODLES

LINDA CUELLAR
RIVERSIDE, CA

This is a quick and tasty meal, very easy to prepare. It's one of my go-to meals. I like to serve an Asian salad with this dish.

12-oz. pkg. thin egg noodles, uncooked
1/2 lb. boneless pork, cubed
1 T. oil
2 lbs. fresh bean sprouts, rinsed and drained
4 to 5 green onions, chopped and divided
2 eggs, beaten
3 T. soy sauce
salt and pepper to taste

1 Cook noodles according to package directions; drain. Meanwhile, in a skillet over medium-high heat, brown pork cubes in oil; drain. Stir in bean sprouts and half of green onions; heat through. Stir eggs into pork mixture; cook until almost done. Stir in soy sauce, salt and pepper. Add cooked noodles; mix well. Sprinkle with remaining onions and serve.

Makes 4 servings

NEWLYWED ROAST

CHARLENE MCCAIN
BAKERSFIELD, CA

Every new bride needs a can't-fail dish, and this is mine...that's why I call it the Newlywed Roast. Simple to prepare, yet delicious enough for the fussiest mother-in-law! I have served it to company for years, and it still gets raves.

1 Place oil in a Dutch oven or other heavy oven-safe pot with a lid. Heat over medium heat. Roll roast in flour until it is coated on all sides. Place roast in hot oil and brown on all sides. Remove from heat.

2 In a bowl, mix together soup, soup mix and water. Pour mixture over roast. Cover pot with lid. Bake at 325 degrees for 3 hours. Remove from oven; arrange vegetables around roast. Return to oven for another 30 minutes, or until vegetables are tender. Transfer roast to a platter; surround with vegetables. Let roast stand for several minutes before slicing.

Makes 8 servings

1 T. oil

3-lb. beef chuck roast, rump roast or 7-bone roast

1/2 c. all-purpose flour

10-3/4 oz. can cream of mushroom soup

1.35-oz. pkg. onion soup mix

1 c. water

8 potatoes, halved or quartered

6 carrots, peeled and chopped

1 onion, quartered

NONNA'S CHRISTMAS EVE SPAGHETTI

SHARON VELENOSI
COSTA MESA, CA

My Nonna made this traditional Christmas Eve dish every year. We couldn't wait to sit down to it! It is one of the special joys and memories of Nonna that we continue every Christmas Eve.

2 7-oz. cans tuna packed in olive oil, drained and oil reserved

2-oz. can flat fillets of anchovies, drained

2 cloves garlic, finely minced

Optional: 1 T. olive oil

28-oz. can tomato purée

32-oz. pkg. spaghetti, uncooked and divided

1 Combine tuna and anchovies in a bowl; finely mince together and set aside.

2 In a skillet over medium heat, sauté garlic in reserved oil until soft. Add tuna mixture; sauté for about 2 minutes, adding the extra olive oil if necessary. Stir in tomato purée. Reduce heat to low. Cover and simmer for 30 minutes, adding a little water if a thinner sauce is desired.

3 Meanwhile, cook 3/4 of spaghetti according to package directions, reserving the rest for another recipe; drain. Serve sauce over cooked spaghetti.

Makes 6 to 8 servings

PARMESAN-CRUSTED CHICKEN

KIMBERLY HANCOCK
MURRIETA, CA

This recipe is so easy, I can make it with my eyes closed...terrific for a busy weeknight. Serve on a bed of spaghetti with marinara sauce.

1 Combine mayonnaise and cheese. Spread mixture over chicken; sprinkle with bread crumbs. Arrange in a lightly greased 13"x9" baking pan. Bake, uncovered, at 425 degrees for 20 minutes, or until chicken juices run clear.

Serves 4

1/2 c. mayonnaise
1/4 c. grated Parmesan cheese
1/4 c. Italian-seasoned dry bread crumbs
4 boneless, skinless chicken breasts

SPINACH PARMESAN ORZO

KATHLEEN STURM
CORONA, CA

This easy side dish is excellent...everyone I have made it for loves it! I like to sauté the spinach early in the day so it's a bit quicker to prepare at dinnertime.

1 Melt 2 tablespoons butter in a large skillet over medium heat. Add garlic; sauté for about 30 seconds, just until lightly golden. Add spinach and salt to skillet.

2 Sauté for a few minutes until spinach is wilted; set aside spinach in a bowl. In the same skillet, melt remaining butter over medium-high heat. Add uncooked pasta; cook and stir until lightly golden. Stir in broth. Reduce heat to low; cover and simmer until orzo is cooked and liquid is almost gone, 10 to 15 minutes. Remove from heat. Add wilted spinach and cheese; toss to combine. Season with salt and pepper.

Serves 6 to 8

4 T. butter, divided
1 T. garlic, chopped
6-oz. pkg. fresh baby spinach
1/8 t. salt
1 c. orzo pasta, uncooked
14-1/2 oz. can chicken broth
1/2 c. shredded Parmesan or Italian-blend cheese
salt and pepper to taste

PENNY'S TURKEY ENCHILADAS

SANDRA SMITH
LANCASTER, CA

Penny is my pen pal in Oklahoma; we've been friends since 1965 and often exchange recipes. A few years ago, I needed a good casserole dish to serve to a houseful of out-of-town guests and she sent me this one. I doubled everything, made two of the casseroles and froze one of them for later on. It was a big hit...thanks, Penny!

8-1/2 oz. jar green enchilada sauce
10-3/4 oz. can cream of chicken soup
2 c. cooked turkey, diced
1 c. onion, diced
2 c. shredded Cheddar or Monterey Jack cheese, divided
6 to 8 corn tortillas
oil for frying
Garnish: salsa, sour cream, guacamole

1 Stir together enchilada sauce and soup in a saucepan over medium-low heat; simmer until heated through. In a separate bowl, mix together turkey, onion and one cup cheese. Pour half of sauce mixture into turkey mixture; stir well and set aside.

2 In a skillet over medium-high heat, fry tortillas in oil, about 5 seconds each, until softened. Drain on paper towels. Spoon turkey mixture onto tortillas and roll up. Place enchiladas, seam-side down, in a 2-quart casserole dish sprayed with non-stick vegetable spray. Spoon remaining sauce mixture over top; sprinkle with remaining cheese.

3 Bake, uncovered, at 350 degrees for 30 to 45 minutes, until hot and bubbly. Serve with desired garnishes.

Serves 6 to 8

NO-FUSS TURKEY & STUFFING

CHARLENE MCCAIN
BAKERSFIELD, CA

I love turkey & stuffing and like to have it more often than just holidays, but who has the time? With my slow cooker and prepared stuffing mix, my family and I can enjoy a scrumptious turkey dinner whenever we want. Pass the cranberry sauce, please!

1/2 c. onion, diced
1/2 c. celery, chopped
3 T. butter, divided
2 6-oz. pkgs. chicken-
flavored stuffing mix
1/2 c. hot water
2 to 3-lb. boneless
turkey breast
1/4 t. poultry seasoning
1/2 t. salt
1/2 t. pepper

1 In a skillet over medium heat, sauté onion and celery in one tablespoon butter, just until translucent. Meanwhile, lightly grease the inside of a 6-quart slow cooker. Spread dry stuffing mix in bottom of crock. Add onion mixture, water and remaining butter; mix well.

2 Place turkey, breast-side up, on top of stuffing mixture; sprinkle with seasonings. Cover and cook on low setting for 6 hours, or until turkey juices run clear. Remove turkey breast from slow cooker to a cutting board. Let stand several minutes before slicing. Gently stir stuffing in crock; transfer to a serving platter. Top stuffing with sliced turkey.

Makes 4 to 6 servings

QUINOA STUFFED PEPPERS

JONI RICK
HEMET, CA

Looking for a way to make stuffed peppers with a healthy dairy-free vegetarian twist, I came up with this tasty blend of flavors. It's easy to fix in a slow cooker. To make this dish kid-friendly, drizzle peppers with your favorite barbecue sauce before serving.

2-1/4 c. water, divided
1 t. salt
1 c. quinoa, uncooked
4-oz. can mushroom pieces, drained
15-oz. can corn, drained
15-oz. can black beans, drained and rinsed
8 green peppers, tops removed

1 In a large saucepan over medium-high heat, bring 2 cups water to a boil. Stir in quinoa and salt. Reduce heat to medium-low. Cover and simmer for 12 to 15 minutes, until all liquid is absorbed. Combine cooked quinoa, mushrooms, corn and beans. Spoon mixture into peppers; arrange in a 6-quart slow cooker. Add remaining water to bottom of slow cooker. Cover and cook on low setting for 4 to 5 hours, until peppers are tender.

Makes 8 servings

TANGY PEACH-GLAZED CHICKEN

KATHLEEN STURM
CORONA, CA

I made this delicious grilled chicken for my sister many years ago. She just had to have the recipe that night! Now she makes it for her family often.

3 lbs. chicken pieces
1 c. peach jam or preserves
2 T. oil
1 T. plus 1 t. soy sauce
1 T. dry mustard
1 clove garlic, minced
1/4 t. cayenne pepper
1 t. salt
1/2 t. pepper

1 Place chicken pieces on an oiled grate over medium-high heat. Grill for 30 to 40 minutes. Meanwhile, combine remaining ingredients in a bowl; mix well. Brush peach mixture generously over chicken during last 10 minutes of cooking. Grill until chicken juices run clear when pierced.

Makes 8 servings

RICH'S CHARCOAL LEMON-LIME CHICKEN

KELLY GREENE
RIVERSIDE, CA

This recipe is my stepdad's. It is always requested when we go to visit him...terrific for tailgating!

1 Place chicken in a large plastic zipping bag; set aside. In a bowl, combine remaining ingredients except oil and garnish. Blend well; whisk in oil. Add marinade to chicken; seal bag. Refrigerate for 8 hours to overnight, turning occasionally.

2 One hour before serving time, bring chicken to room temperature, discarding marinade. Place chicken on an oiled grate over medium-high heat. Grill for 4 minutes per side, or until chicken juices run clear. Garnish as desired.

Serves 6

6 boneless, skinless chicken breasts
1/2 c. brown sugar, packed
1/4 c. cider vinegar
3 T. coarse mustard
juice of 1 lime
juice of 1/2 lemon
3 cloves garlic, pressed
1-1/2 t. salt, or to taste
pepper to taste
6 T. oil
Garnish: lemon slices, chopped fresh herbs

CHAPTER FIVE

CASUAL & COOL

Nibbles & Sips

WHETHER YOU ARE HAVING AN IMPROMPTU PARTY BY THE POOL OR A MUCH-ANTICIPATED GET-TOGETHER ON THE SUN PORCH, THESE APPETIZER AND PARTY RECIPES ARE SURE TO MAKE IT A COOL CALIFORNIA EVENT.

3-CHEESE BEER FONDUE

SONYA LABBE
LOS ANGELES, CA

Each time I want to slow down, I serve a fondue. It encourages everybody to take it slow and to enjoy the food and each other's company, California style.

1/2 head cauliflower, cut into flowerets

1/2 bunch broccoli, cut into flowerets

1 c. shredded Cheddar cheese

1 c. shredded Gruyère cheese

1 c. shredded Swiss cheese

1 T. all-purpose flour

1-1/2 c. beer or non-alcoholic beer

2 T. Dijon mustard

1 baguette loaf, cubed

1 Bring a large saucepan of water to a boil over medium-high heat. Add cauliflower and broccoli to pot; cook for 2 minutes. Drain, rinse in cold water and set aside. In a bowl, combine cheeses and flour; toss to mix and set aside.

2 Pour beer into a small saucepan and bring to a simmer over medium heat. Reduce heat to low and add cheese mixture, a little at a time, stirring constantly. After cheese is melted, add mustard. Transfer cheese mixture to a warm fondue pot. Arrange cauliflower, broccoli and baguette pieces around fondue pot for dipping.

Serves 6

APRICOT-ALMOND BRIE

LINDA WHELAN
OCEANSIDE, CA

Rich and creamy and with an elegant presentation. This is terrific because it's fast and easy.

1 Remove top rind from cheese. Place cheese on a serving plate; set aside. In a small saucepan over low heat, combine preserves and liqueur. Heat until hot, but do not boil. Spoon sauce over cheese; sprinkle with almonds. Serve with crackers.

Serves 6 to 8

8-oz. wedge Brie cheese
1/2 c. apricot preserves
1 T. orange-flavored
  liqueur
1 T. sliced almonds,
  toasted
buttery round crackers

PAMELA'S TARTAR SAUCE

PAMELA BENNETT
WHITTIER, CA

When I was a young adult, fish was a very scary food! My husband and kids really liked frozen fish sticks. I did too, but something just seemed to be missing. I played with various tartar sauce recipes and came up with this one! Now I serve many types of fresh fish for dinner. For the zingiest flavor, use fresh-squeezed lemon juice.

1 In a small container with a lid, mix all ingredients well. Cover and refrigerate up to one week. Serve with fish.

Makes 4 to 6 servings

1 c. mayonnaise
3 T. sweet pickle relish
3 T. onion, finely
  chopped
3 T. catsup
3 T. lemon juice
2 t. dill weed

BARBECUED ONION RELISH

CHARMIE FISHER
FONTANA, CA

This recipe came from my mother-in-law. She shared it with me at one of our family barbecues, and I've kept it ever since. It's so yummy on everything grilled! I especially like it on grilled sausages.

3 T. canola oil
4 onions, halved and
  sliced
1 T. sugar
1/2 t. salt
4 cloves garlic, chopped
1 T. chili powder
1/4 t. red pepper flakes
1/2 c. hickory-flavored
  barbecue sauce
1/2 c. beer or chicken
  broth
1 T. molasses
1 T. Dijon mustard
1 T. red wine vinegar
2-1/2 t. soy sauce

1 Heat oil in a large saucepan over medium heat. Add onions; sprinkle with sugar and salt. Cover and cook, stirring occasionally, until onions are soft and juicy, but not browned, about 30 minutes. Add garlic, chili powder and red pepper flakes. Sauté for 4 minutes. Stir in remaining ingredients; reduce heat.

2 Simmer, uncovered, stirring occasionally, until mixture thickens slightly, about 10 minutes. Cool to room temperature. Cover tightly and refrigerate for 24 hours to allow flavors to develop. May be made up to one week ahead. To serve warm, simmer over low heat.

Makes 8 servings

KITCHEN TIP

Keep slices of lemon and lime in a sealed container in your fridge for a touch of citrus in drinks and special dishes.

SPICY BUFFALO CHICKEN WINGS

ROSALYN ODION
YORBA LINDA, CA

Serve with celery and blue cheese dressing.

1 Arrange chicken in a greased 13"x9" baking pan; bake at 425 degrees for one hour, turning frequently. Remove from oven; set aside. Whisk hot sauce, butter and vinegar together; pour over chicken. Toss gently to coat.

Serves 4 to 6

2-1/2 lbs. chicken wings
4-oz. bottle hot pepper sauce
1/2 c. butter, melted
2 T. white vinegar

QUICK PICNIC PICKLES

LISA SETT
THOUSAND OAKS, CA

Jars of these fresh veggie pickles make great gifts to share with friends & neighbors.

1 Combine vinegar and sugar in canning jar. Shake to mix well. Add vegetables and cilantro to jar in small layers and pack to top. Fill with water to cover vegetables. Replace lid; seal tightly. Turn over jar to mix well. Refrigerate overnight before using. May store in refrigerator for up to one week.

Makes one jar

1/2 c. rice vinegar
1/2 c. sugar
1-quart wide-mouth canning jar and lid, sterilized
2 cucumbers, peeled and thinly sliced
1/2 red, orange or yellow pepper, cut into long strips
1/8 red onion, cut into wedges or strips
1 carrot, peeled and thinly sliced
1 T. fresh cilantro, chopped

CALIFORNIA DREAM SMOOTHIES

SONYA LABBE
WEST HOLLYWOOD, CA

This is what California is all about...sunshine and dreams. You'll love this delicious creamy drink. Kids love it too!

6-oz. can frozen orange juice concentrate
1 c. milk
1/2 c. half-and-half
1/4 c. powdered sugar
1 t. vanilla extract
1-1/2 c. ice cubes

1 In a blender, combine all ingredients. Process until smooth. Divide into 4 glasses.

Makes 4 servings

PICNIC PINWHEELS

KIMBERLY HANCOCK
MURRIETA, CA

These roll-ups are lots of fun for kids, and moms as well, because they can be made in just minutes. It's a great spin on our old standby, the peanut butter & jelly sandwich. Crunchy apple can be substituted for the banana too. Yummy!

1/3 c. creamy peanut butter
4 8-inch flour tortillas
1 c. banana, chopped
1/4 c. granola cereal

1 Spread peanut butter on each tortilla; top with banana and granola. Tightly roll up tortillas and cut each one in half. Wrap roll-ups in plastic wrap or aluminum foil to pack in lunchboxes.

Serves 4

CALIFORNIA SPINACH SNACKERS

KIMBERLY HANCOCK
MURRIETA, CA

These are so tasty, sometimes I make two batches because they go so fast!

1 Melt butter in a saucepan over medium heat. Add onion and cook until tender; drain. In a bowl, combine onion, spinach, mayonnaise, cheese and nutmeg; set aside.

2 Unroll biscuit dough; divide each in half horizontally. Press biscuit halves into lightly greased mini muffin cups. Shape each into small cups that extend slightly beyond the rim. Fill with spinach mixture. Bake at 375 degrees for 12 minutes, or until biscuits are lightly golden. Serve warm or at room temperature.

Makes 16

1 T. butter
1/2 c. onion, finely chopped
10-oz. pkg. frozen chopped spinach, thawed
3/4 c. mayonnaise
8-oz. pkg. shredded mozzarella cheese
1-1/2 t. nutmeg
16.3-oz. tube refrigerated buttermilk biscuits
salt and pepper to taste

CALIFORNIA COOL

Smoothies, with all kinds of variations, were born in Southern California and are available at a number of spots. They are healthy, nutritious and downright fun to make and enjoy.

CHEESE STRAWS

JUDY BORECKY
ESCONDIDO, CA

To make these addictive nibbles even more quickly, shred the cheese in the food processor before you begin.

2 c. all-purpose flour
2 c. shredded extra-
  sharp Cheddar cheese
1 t. baking powder
1/2 t. salt
6 T. ice water
1 c. butter, softened

1 Combine all ingredients in a food processor or heavy-duty mixer; chill. Roll out to 1/4-inch thickness; cut into 2"x1/2" strips. Arrange on ungreased baking sheets; bake at 350 degrees for 10 to 12 minutes.

Serves 4

SLOW-COOKED SCRUMPTIOUS SALSA

MARLENE DARNELL
NEWPORT BEACH, CA

Nothing beats the taste of fresh, homemade salsa. This recipe is so simple, I make it all the time with fresh produce from my backyard garden. I give it as gifts and make sure to pass the recipe along with it!

10 roma tomatoes, cored
2 cloves garlic
1 onion, cut into wedges
2 jalapeño peppers,
  seeded and chopped
1/4 c. fresh cilantro,
  coarsely chopped
1/2 t. salt

1 Combine tomatoes, garlic and onion in a slow cooker. Cover and cook on high setting for 2-1/2 to 3 hours, until vegetables are tender. Remove crock and let cool. Combine cooled tomato mixture and remaining ingredients in a food processor or blender. Process to desired consistency. May be refrigerated in a covered container for about one week.

Makes about 2 cups

VICKIE'S FAVORITE GUACAMOLE

VICKIE
GOOSEBERRY PATCH

Whenever we have a Mexican-themed potluck, I'm requested to bring my homemade guacamole. It's almost foolproof and oh-so-good!

1 Scoop pulp out of avocados into a bowl. Mash to desired consistency with a potato masher. Add remaining ingredients; mix well. Serve with your favorite tortilla chips.

Makes 2 cups

4 avocados, halved and pitted
1 onion, chopped
2 cloves garlic, minced
2 T. lime juice
1/8 t. kosher salt
tortilla chips

BONUS IDEA

Choosing the perfect avocado can be daunting. The avocado should be firm but yield to gentle pressure and it should have a slightly bumpy texture. Color can vary, but usually the darker ones are riper.

PRETZEL TWISTS

MARLENE DARNELL
NEWPORT BEACH, CA

Try shaping the pretzels into letters or numbers for a fun twist!

2 16-oz. loaves frozen
  bread dough, thawed
1 egg white, beaten
1 t. water
coarse salt to taste

1 Divide dough into twenty-four, 1-1/2 inch balls. Roll each ball into a rope 14 inches long. Shape as desired; arrange one inch apart on lightly greased baking sheets. Let rise in a warm place for 20 minutes. Whisk together egg white and water; brush over pretzels. Sprinkle with salt. Place a shallow pan with one inch of boiling water on bottom rack of oven. Bake pretzels on rack above water at 350 degrees for 20 minutes, or until golden.

Makes 2 dozen

OLD-FASHIONED MOVIE POPCORN

LAURA SLATER
BAKERSFIELD, CA

So much better tasting than microwave popcorn. Try sprinkling with grated Parmesan cheese, seasoning salt or sugar.

1/4 c. oil
1/4 c. unpopped popcorn
2 T. butter, melted
1 t. salt

1 Heat oil in a heavy saucepan over medium-high heat. Add popcorn and cover. Once popping begins, gently shake the pan by moving it back and forth over the burner. Keep the lid slightly ajar to let steam escape. Once popping slows to several seconds between pops, remove pan from heat and pour popcorn into a large bowl. Drizzle with butter; add salt to taste.

Makes about 8 cups

CRANBERRY SLUSH

JUDY BORECKY
ESCONDIDO, CA

Create a festive garnish for each glass…just slip the cranberries and orange and lime slices onto wooden skewers.

1 Combine sugar and 2 cups water in a large saucepan over medium heat, stirring until sugar dissolves. Add grape juice, frozen fruit concentrates and remaining 6 cups water. Pour into 2 one-gallon-size heavy-duty plastic zipping bags; freeze until solid.

2 To serve, place frozen mixture into a punch bowl; pour chilled lemon-lime soda over mixture. Stir to break up chunks until mixture is slushy. Garnish each individual serving, as desired.

Makes about 6 quarts

3/4 c. sugar

8 c. water, divided

2 c. white grape juice

12-oz. can frozen orange juice concentrate

12-oz. can frozen cranberry juice cocktail concentrate

6-oz. can frozen limeade concentrate

2-ltr. bottle lemon-lime soda, chilled

1/4 t. pepper

2 T. butter, sliced

Garnishes: fresh cranberries, orange slices, lime slices

KITCHEN TIP

Make special ice cubes for your iced beverages by adding fresh cranberries, lime peel or cherries with the water in the ice cube trays before freezing.

MOM'S STRAWBERRY LEMONADE

**KATHLEEN STURM
CORONA, CA**

Here in southern California, we're lucky to have a lemon tree in our backyard. This refreshing thirst quencher is a staple in our fridge during the hot summer months.

2 c. lemon juice
2 c. sugar
1 c. strawberries, hulled and puréed

1 In a one-gallon jug or pitcher, combine lemon juice, sugar and puréed strawberries. Mix to start dissolving sugar. Add enough water to fill jug. Stir until sugar is dissolved completely. Chill; serve ice-cold.

Makes one gallon

EASY SLOW-COOKER BEAN DIP

**MARNI SENNER
LONG BEACH, CA**

This dip is perfect to tote to potlucks and family gatherings.

4 16-oz. cans refried beans
1-lb. pkg. Colby Jack cheese, cubed
1-1/4 oz. pkg. taco seasoning mix
1 bunch green onions, chopped
1 c. sour cream
8-oz. pkg. cream cheese, cubed

1 Place all ingredients in a 3-1/2-quart slow cooker; stir to mix. Cover and cook on low setting for about 2-1/2 hours. Stir often.

Makes 11 cups

FILLED CHEESE PUFFS

JO ANN
GOOSEBERRY PATCH

These mini cream puffs are perfect for a ladies' luncheon. Spoon in your favorite filling like finely chopped chicken or shrimp salad. Delicious and so pretty on a party table.

1 In a saucepan, combine water, butter, salt and pepper. Bring to a boil over medium-high heat. Add flour; stir with a wooden spoon until dough forms.

2 Transfer dough to a large bowl. With an electric mixer on high speed, beat in eggs, adding one at a time, beating well after each. Beat until smooth and cooled; beat in cheese.

3 Drop batter by tablespoonfuls, one-inch apart, onto buttered baking sheets. With moistened fingers, smooth tops. Bake at 400 degrees for 25 to 30 minutes, until puffed and golden. Place baking sheets on wire racks until puffs are cool. Slice off top 1/3 of each puff; pull out the doughy centers. Spoon in filling; replace tops of puffs.

Serves 8

1 c. water
3 T. butter, sliced
3/4 t. salt
1/2 t. pepper
1 c. all-purpose flour
4 eggs
1/2 c. Gruyère cheese, finely shredded
1 c. favorite filling

HAM & GRUYÈRE EGG CUPS

SONYA LABBE
SANTA MONICA, CA

This recipe is always a favorite and is easy, simple and tasty. It's very pretty too!

12 thin slices deli ham
3/4 c. shredded Gruyère cheese
1 doz. eggs
salt and pepper to taste
1 c. half-and-half
2 T. grated Parmesan cheese

1 Spray a muffin tin with non-stick vegetable spray. Line each muffin cup with a slice of ham folded in half. Top each ham slice with one tablespoon Gruyère cheese, an egg cracked into the cup, a sprinkle of salt and pepper, one tablespoon half-and-half and 1/2 teaspoon Parmesan cheese.

2 Place muffin tin on a baking sheet. Bake at 450 degrees for 15 minutes, until eggs are set. Allow baked eggs to cool for several minutes before removing them from the muffin tin.

Makes one dozen

TANGY DEVILED EGGS

JO ANN
GOOSEBERRY PATCH

No family reunion is complete without deviled eggs!

4 eggs, hard-boiled and peeled
1 t. prepared horseradish
1 t. onion, minced
1/3 c. light mayonnaise
1/4 t. celery salt
Garnish: sliced green onion

1 Slice eggs in half lengthwise and remove yolks. Mince yolks in a small mixing bowl; combine with horseradish, onion, mayonnaise and salt. Spoon mixture into egg white halves; keep chilled. Garnish as desired.

Makes 8 servings

124   ALL-TIME-FAVORITE RECIPES FROM *California* SOUTHERN CALIFORNIA COOKS - - - -

HAWAIIAN WINGS

YVONNE VAN BRIMMER
APPLE VALLEY, CA

I like to bring the taste of the islands to our parties. This simple recipe has no last-minute prep so you can enjoy your friends! Tasty served as an appetizer or over steamed rice for dinner.

1 Place wings in a large slow cooker. Top with onion, soy sauce, pineapple with juice, garlic and ginger. Toss gently to coat. Cover and cook on low setting for 8 hours, or until wings are no longer pink in the center. Sprinkle with coconut, if desired.

Makes 6 to 8 servings

4 to 5 lbs. frozen chicken wings, thawed

1 onion, chopped

1/3 c. soy sauce

20-oz. can pineapple chunks

granulated garlic to taste

2 t. ground ginger

Optional: shredded coconut

CALIFORNIA COOL

Thirsty? The tiki-style Mai Tai has a slightly disputed origin in Southern California. Two restaurants, Trader Vic's and Don the Beachcomber, both claim ownership. For a non-alcoholic drink, Orange Lemonade combines two citrus fruits for a refreshing taste. And, yes, there's even a town named Citrus.

HOLIDAY WASSAIL

PAMELA BENNETT
WHITTIER, CA

More than 20 years ago, I received this recipe from a stranger at the grocery store. I had asked her an opinion on an item I was considering for my annual Christmas party. She proceeded to share this recipe with me. I was so excited to try it. I made it for my party and it was a huge hit...so tasty! I've made it many times since, usually adding the wine. A favorite every time. And there's always requests for the recipe!

1 gal. apple cider
1 c. light brown sugar, packed
6-oz. can frozen lemonade concentrate
6-oz. can frozen orange juice concentrate
12 whole cloves
6 whole allspice
4 4-inch cinnamon sticks
1 t. ground nutmeg
Optional: 750-ml. bottle port wine

1 Combine cider, brown sugar and juices in a large pot over medium heat; stir well. Divide spices evenly between 2 empty family-size tea bags or small muslin spice bags; tie closed with thread.

2 Add spice bags to pot with cider mixture; simmer about 20 minutes. Add a little water if liquid seems too thick. Transfer to a 6 to 7-quart slow cooker. Add wine if using; cover and warm through on low setting. Keep warm on low setting for serving.

Serves 15

HONEY SESAME WINGS

KIMBERLY HANCOCK
MURRIETA, CA

Always a hit with young & old alike...these wings are sweet and tangy, but not too spicy. We just love 'em!

1 Place chicken wings on an ungreased broiler pan; sprinkle with salt and pepper. Place pan 4 to 5 inches under broiler. Broil for 10 minutes on each side, or until chicken is golden. Transfer wings to a slow cooker. Combine remaining ingredients except sesame seed; pour over wings. Cover and cook on low setting for 4 to 5 hours, or on high setting for 2 to 2-1/2 hours. Arrange on a serving platter; sprinkle with sesame seed.

Makes about 2-1/2 dozen

> 3 lbs. chicken wings
> salt and pepper to taste
> 2 c. honey
> 1 c. soy sauce
> 1/2 c. catsup
> 1/4 c. oil
> 2 cloves garlic, minced
> Garnish: sesame seed

ROSEMARY-WHITE BEAN DIP

JOANN
GOOSEBERRY PATCH

Rosemary is one of my favorite herbs, so I always have a couple pots of it growing in a pot on my windowsill. A good friend shared this recipe with me, and I just knew I had to try it. So one game day I whipped up a batch, and was it a hit!

1 Combine beans, garlic, rosemary, pepper flakes and broth in a medium slow cooker. Cover and cook on high setting for 3 hours, or until beans are soft and liquid is mostly absorbed. Remove crock and cool. Place cooled bean mixture into a blender; stir in oil and lemon juice. Process until dip reaches desired consistency. Spoon dip into a serving bowl; sprinkle with parsley. Serve with dippers.

Serves 4 to 6

> 3/4 c. dried white beans
> 4 cloves garlic, minced
> 1 T. fresh rosemary, chopped
> 1 t. red pepper flakes
> 2 c. vegetable broth
> salt to taste
> 7 T. olive oil
> 1-1/2 T. lemon juice
> 1 T. fresh parsley, chopped
> assorted dippers such as crackers, toasted baguette slices and cherry tomatoes

HOT CARAMEL APPLE CIDER

**KIMBERLY HANCOCK
MURRIETA, CA**

A perfect warmer-upper for a chilly fall day. Put the cider on to simmer, go out for a hayride or an afternoon of apple picking, and when you get home the scent of this cider will have filled the whole house! What could be better?

1/2 gal. apple cider
1/2 c. brown sugar, packed
1-1/2 t. cider vinegar
1 t. vanilla extract
4-inch cinnamon stick
6 whole cloves
1 orange, thinly sliced
Garnish: caramel ice cream topping

1 Combine all ingredients except caramel topping in a slow cooker. Cover and cook on low setting for 5 to 6 hours. Discard orange slices and spices. Serve cider in hot mugs, drizzling a teaspoon of caramel topping into each mug.

Makes 16 servings

BONUS IDEA

Serve Hot Caramel Apple Cider with homemade (or favorite store-bought) crackers and cheese for a savory pairing with the sweet cider.

MARINATED GARLIC OLIVES

SHARON VELENOSI
COSTA MESA, CA

A few simple ingredients can do wonders for ordinary canned olives...you'll be amazed at the flavor!

1 In a wide-mouthed jar with a lid, combine all ingredients except oil. Add enough oil to cover ingredients. Secure lid. Refrigerate at least 24 hours to blend flavors before serving.

Makes 2 cups

2 c. green olives,
  drained
1 to 2 cloves garlic,
  slivered
3 thin slices lemon
1 t. whole peppercorns
3 bay leaves
1/4 c. wine vinegar
1/4 to 1/2 c. olive oil

UNCLE PICKLE & AUNT T'S FAVORITE TOMATILLO SALSA

REBECCA GONZALEZ
MORENO VALLEY, CA

This is a salsa my best friends and I love! We live far from each other now, but when we get together, I make sure I have plenty of this salsa on hand to enjoy with chips. Enjoy it as a condiment too.

1 Add all ingredients except salt to a large saucepan; cover with water. Bring to a boil over high heat; reduce heat to medium. Boil for 15 minutes, or until tomatillos start to split open. With a slotted spoon, remove all ingredients and add to a blender. Process until smooth; season with salt. Cool before serving; cover and keep refrigerated.

Makes 12 to 15 servings

12 tomatillos, husks
  removed
1 onion, peeled and
  quartered
3 to 4 serrano chiles, to
  taste
3 to 4 cloves garlic,
  peeled
salt to taste

MEXICAN COFFEE

CHARLENE MCCAIN
BAKERSFIELD, CA

After a day of shopping, I like to put my feet up and relax with a cup of hot Mexican coffee. It is so sweet and good. This makes plenty, so share it with friends!

10 c. water
1/2 c. ground coffee, or more to taste
1 c. brown sugar, packed
1/2 c. chocolate syrup
1/4 t. cinnamon
1 c. milk
1/8 t. salt

1 Pour water into a 14-cup coffee maker. Add ground coffee to basket; add remaining ingredients to pot. Brew as usual. Stir well before serving.

Makes 14 servings

NOTE: If coffee maker is smaller than 14 cups, use 9 cups water, 3/4 cup brown sugar and 1/2 cup milk; other ingredients are unchanged.

CALIFORNIA COOL

Yes, there really is a ranch surrounding Hidden Valley® Ranch Dressing. In 1954 a cowboy from Nebraska, Steve Henson and his wife Gayle, developed a dude ranch near Santa Barbara. Steve kept experimenting with a buttermilk-based dressing, and it took off. The rest, of course, is tasty history.

MINI BEAN DIP JARS

SONYA LABBE
WEST HOLLYWOOD, CA

I came up with this recipe for my uncle, who prefers not to share a communal dip bowl. Now, everybody can enjoy their own yummy cup of dip. Use plastic containers if you prefer...terrific for tucking into lunchboxes!

1 In a bowl, mix tomatoes with onion and salt; set aside. In a separate bowl, mash avocados with jalapeños, lime juice and 2 tablespoons sour cream. In the bottom of each jar, spread a half-inch layer of refried beans.

2 Layer each jar with 2 tablespoons cheese, one tablespoon tomato mixture, 3 tablespoons avocado mixture, 2 tablespoons sour cream and 2 tablespoons olives. Add lids, if not serving immediately. Serve with tortilla chips.

Makes 8 servings

2 tomatoes, finely chopped

1/2 c. onion, finely chopped

1/2 t. coarse salt

2 ripe avocados, halved, pitted and peeled

1 to 2 pickled jalapeño peppers, minced

1 T. lime juice

1 c. plus 2 T. sour cream, divided

2 16-oz. cans refried beans

1 c. shredded Cheddar cheese

6-oz. can chopped black olives, drained

8 8-oz. canning jars with lids

tortilla chips

CHAPTER SIX

CALIFORNIA DREAMING
Desserts

YOU WOULDN'T DREAM OF
ENDING A MEAL WITHOUT JUST
A LITTLE SOMETHING SWEET,
AND THESE DELICIOUS DISHES
ARE SURE TO PUT THE ICING ON
THE CAKE.

AUTUMN PUMPKIN BARS

JESSICA JACOBY
TEMECULA, CA

*Every year on September 1st, I make a batch of these bars.
I continue to make them through the holidays. We love them!*

2 c. canned pumpkin
1 c. oil or applesauce
4 eggs, beaten
1 t. vanilla extract
2 c. sugar
2 c. all-purpose flour
1 t. baking soda
1 t. salt
2 t. cinnamon
1 t. ground ginger
1/2 t. ground cloves

1 In a large bowl, whisk together pumpkin, oil or applesauce, eggs and vanilla; set aside. In a separate bowl, combine remaining ingredients; mix well and stir into pumpkin mixture. Spread in an ungreased 13"x9" baking pan. Bake at 350 degrees for 20 to 25 minutes. Cool; cut into bars.

Makes 3 dozen

ZUCCHINI BROWNIES

LISA SETT
THOUSAND OAKS, CA

*These rich chocolate brownies have two kinds of chocolate. They
also have lots of grated zucchini, plus applesauce to replace some
of the oil. So, they're healthier than usual...don't tell the kids!*

2 c. all-purpose flour
1-1/4 c. sugar
1/2 c. baking cocoa
1-1/2 t. baking soda
1 t. salt
1/4 c. oil
1/4 c. unsweetened
  applesauce
1 egg, beaten
1 T. vanilla extract
2 c. zucchini, grated and
  drained
1 c. semi-sweet chocolate
  chips
Optional: powdered
  sugar

1 In a bowl, combine flour, sugar, cocoa, baking soda and salt; mix well. In a separate large bowl, mix together oil, applesauce, egg and vanilla. Add flour mixture to oil mixture; stir until well mixed. Batter will be thick.

2 Fold in zucchini and chocolate chips. Spray a 13"x9" baking pan with non-stick vegetable spray; dust with cocoa. Spread batter in pan. Bake at 350 degrees for 20 to 25 minutes. Cut into squares; serve plain or dust with powdered sugar.

Makes 12 to 15 brownies

BORECKY PUDDING COOKIES

JUDY BORECKY
ESCONDIDO, CA

These cookies are easy to make. Back in the early 1960s, I made them for our sons all the time. You can change the flavor of the pudding to make cookies in colors for any holiday.

1 In a bowl, combine butter, eggs, dry pudding mix, sugar, vanilla, flour, baking soda, cream of tartar and salt. Beat with an electric mixer on medium speed, just until blended. Stir in nuts and coconut, if using.

2 Drop dough onto ungreased baking sheets, 2 tablespoons per cookie. Bake at 350 degrees for 14 minutes, or until lightly golden. Cool completely; decorate with Vanilla Glaze. May top cookies with a colored jelly bean, for example, white jelly beans for coconut cookies.

Makes 3-1/2 dozen

1 c. butter, softened
2 eggs
2 3-oz. pkgs. instant pudding mix (coconut, chocolate, lemon, pistachio or butterscotch)
1/4 c. sugar
1 t. vanilla extract
2 c. all-purpose flour
1 t. baking soda
1 t. cream of tartar
1/4 t. salt
1/2 c. chopped walnuts or pecans
Optional: 1/2 c. sweetened flaked coconut
Optional: jelly beans

1 Heat butter with half-and-half; remove from heat. Add remaining ingredients; whisk until smooth. Let stand for about 10 minutes; drizzle or spoon over cookies.

VANILLA GLAZE:
1/4 c. butter, sliced
3 T. half-and-half
1/8 t. salt
2 c. powdered sugar
1 t. vanilla extract

CINNAMON & GINGER TREATS

DEBBIE ISAACSON
IRVINE, CA

You won't be able to stop nibbling on these.

3 c. assorted nuts
1 egg white
1 T. orange juice
2/3 c. sugar
1 t. cinnamon
1/2 t. ground ginger
1/2 t. allspice
1/4 t. salt

1 Place nuts in a large mixing bowl; set aside. Blend egg white and orange juice together until frothy; mix in remaining ingredients. Pour over nuts; mix thoroughly. Spread coated nuts onto an aluminum foil-lined baking sheet; bake at 275 degrees for 45 minutes, stirring every 15 minutes. Cool; store in an airtight container.

Makes 3 cups

SWEET VANILLA PUDDING

ELIZABETH CISNEROS
CHINO HILLS, CA

There's nothing more comforting than a bowl of warm homemade pudding!

1/4 c. sugar
2 T. cornstarch
1/8 t. salt
2 c. milk
2 egg yolks, beaten
1 T. butter
2 t. vanilla extract
1/4 t. nutmeg

1 In a small saucepan, combine sugar, cornstarch and salt. Stir in milk; cook and stir over medium heat until thickened. Reduce heat to low; continue cooking and stirring for 2 minutes. Place egg yolks in a small bowl. Add a small amount of hot milk mixture to yolks; stir and return all of yolk mixture to pan, stirring constantly. Bring to a gentle boil; cook and stir one minute longer.

2 Remove from heat; add butter, vanilla and nutmeg. Let cool in pan for 15 minutes, stirring every 5 minutes. Transfer to dessert bowls; cover and refrigerate. May be served slightly warm or cold.

Serves 4

GRANDMA & KATIE'S FROZEN DESSERT

JENNIFER BROWN
GARDEN GROVE, CA

Refreshing during the summer, or any time of year, this tasty treat can be made ahead of time.

1 Blend together peanut butter and corn syrup in a large bowl. Add cereals; stir until coated. Press into the bottom of an ungreased 13"x9" baking pan.

2 Spread ice cream over cereal mixture; sprinkle with peanuts. Swirl chocolate syrup over top. Cover with foil; freeze at least 4 hours before serving. Cut into squares to serve.

Serves 15 to 18

1/2 c. creamy peanut butter
1/2 c. light corn syrup
2 c. crispy rice cereal
2 c. chocolate-flavored crispy rice cereal
1/2 gal. vanilla ice cream, softened
1/2 to 1 c. Spanish peanuts, coarsely chopped
Garnish: chocolate syrup

HONEY PUMPKIN PIE

SHARON VELENOSI
COSTA MESA, CA

Since my husband must avoid refined sugar, I've tried to make his favorite recipes using honey. This is a new version of one of his favorites.

1 In a bowl, beat eggs slightly. Add remaining ingredients except crust; stir well. Pour mixture into unbaked pie crust.

2 Bake at 425 degrees for 15 minutes. Reduce heat to 350 degrees; bake an additional 45 minutes, or until filling is set. Cool; garnish with whipped cream.

Makes 8 servings

2 eggs
15-oz. can pumpkin
3/4 c. honey
1/2 t. salt
1 t. cinnamon
1/2 t. ground ginger
1/8 t. ground cloves
1 c. evaporated milk
9-inch pie crust, unbaked
Garnish: whipped cream

GRANDMA'S CHOCOLATE BON-BONS

SUSAN JACOBS
VISTA, CA

My husband's grandmother gave me a recipe booklet compiled by the Jefferson Volunteer Fire Company Ladies Auxiliary in 1974. In the booklet was Grandma's own recipe for these chocolate bon-bons. For the next 20 years or so, I made these for Christmas, giving them as gifts and serving at family gatherings. Recently everyone misses them, so I thought I'd make them again this year. These are a great gift or cookie swap treat.

1 c. graham cracker crumbs

16-oz. pkg. powdered sugar

1 c. sweetened flaked coconut

1 c. butter, softened

1-1/2 c. creamy peanut butter

12-oz. pkg. semi-sweet chocolate chips

2 T. shortening

1 In a large bowl, combine cracker crumbs, powdered sugar and coconut. Add butter and peanut butter; mix well. Roll mixture into walnut-size balls. Place balls on wax paper; refrigerate until ready to dip in chocolate.

2 Melt chocolate chips with shortening in the top of a double boiler over hot water. Stir until chocolate is melted and smooth. With a fork, dip bon-bons into chocolate, one at a time, coating well. Remove bon-bons to a sheet of wax paper. Return to refrigerator until firm.

Makes 4 dozen

THE BEST BLONDIES

ELIZABETH CISNEROS
CHINO HILLS, CA

For an extra-special dessert, serve topped with a scoop of butter brickle ice cream...delicious.

1 Line the bottom of a 12"x9" baking pan with parchment paper. Spray sides of pan with non-stick vegetable spray and set aside. In a large bowl, mix together butter and brown sugar. Beat in eggs and vanilla until smooth. Stir in flour, baking powder and salt; mix in remaining ingredients.

2 Pour into prepared pan and spread evenly. Bake at 375 degrees for 30 to 40 minutes, until set in the middle. Allow to cool in pan before cutting into bars.

Makes one dozen

1 c. butter, melted and
    slightly cooled
2 c. brown sugar, packed
2 eggs, beaten
2 t. vanilla extract
2 c. all-purpose flour
1/2 t. baking powder
1/4 t. salt
1 c. chopped pecans
1 c. white chocolate chips
3/4 c. toffee or caramel
    baking bits

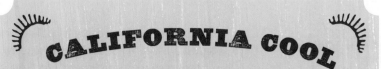

CALIFORNIA COOL

Rocky Road ice cream started its popularity run in 1929 in Oakland, during the Great Depression. Until that point, ice cream choices were vanilla, chocolate and strawberry. This concoction of chocolate ice cream, marshmallows and nuts was an instant hit.

HONEY DATE BARS

MARIAN BUCKLEY
FONTANA, CA

When I was growing up, I always loved seeing a familiar wax paper-wrapped packet in my school lunchbox. It meant that Grammy had baked these yummy cookie bars just for me.

3 eggs, room
  temperature
1 c. honey
1 c. all-purpose flour
1 t. baking powder
1/2 t. salt
2 T. oil
1 T. lemon juice
1 t. vanilla extract
2 c. chopped dates
1 c. chopped walnuts
1 T. lemon zest

1 In a large bowl, beat eggs well. Drizzle in honey while still beating; set aside. In a separate bowl, mix flour, baking powder and salt. Add half of flour mixture to egg mixture along with oil, lemon juice and vanilla; stir well. Add dates, walnuts and lemon zest to remaining flour mixture; toss to coat and add to egg mixture. Stir until dough forms.

2 Spread dough evenly in a lightly greased and floured 13"x9" baking pan. Bake at 350 degrees for 30 to 40 minutes, until golden. Cool in pan on a wire rack. Cut into 24 squares.

Makes 2 dozen

AUTUMN SPICE STREUSEL CAKE

ELLIE LEVESQUE
UPLAND, CA

This is a family favorite. I make it in October because it has the flavors of fall. It's a hit with my Bible study group too!

18-1/4 oz. pkg. spice cake
  mix
1 sleeve graham
  crackers, crushed
3/4 c. brown sugar,
  packed
1/2 c. butter, melted
2 t. cinnamon
Garnish: powdered
  sugar

1 Prepare cake mix according to package directions; set aside batter. In a separate small bowl, mix graham cracker crumbs, brown sugar, butter and cinnamon; set aside. Lightly coat a 12-cup Bundt® pan with non-stick vegetable spray. Pour half of batter into pan. Add all of crumb mixture; pour remaining batter on top. Bake at 350 degrees for 35 to 40 minutes, until cake tests done with a toothpick. Let cool. Turn out cake onto a cake plate; dust with powdered sugar.

Serves 8 to 10

SWEET RASPBERRY-OAT BARS

KATHLEEN STURM
CORONA, CA

My mom used to make these every year for Christmas. Now I add these yummy bars to the cookie tins I share with my neighbors each holiday season.

1 In a large bowl, blend together butter and brown sugar until fluffy; set aside. Combine flour, baking soda and salt in a separate bowl. Stir flour mixture into butter mixture. Add oats and water; mix together until crumbly.

2 Firmly pat half of oat mixture into the bottom of a greased 13"x9" baking pan. In a small bowl, stir together jam and lemon juice; spread over oat mixture. Sprinkle remaining oat mixture over top. Bake at 350 degrees for 25 minutes. Cool completely before cutting into bars.

Makes about 2-1/2 dozen

- 1/2 c. butter
- 1 c. brown sugar, packed
- 1-1/2 c. all-purpose flour
- 1/2 t. baking soda
- 1/2 t. salt
- 1-1/2 c. long-cooking oats, uncooked
- 1/4 c. water
- 2/3 c. seedless raspberry jam
- 1 t. lemon juice

TRIED & TRUE BUNDT CAKE

ELIZABETH CISNEROS
EASTVALE, CA

This recipe never fails...it has won blue ribbons at the county fair several times!

1 In a bowl, beat butter and cream cheese with an electric mixer on medium speed until creamy. Gradually add sugar, beating well. Beat in eggs, one at a time. In a separate bowl, combine flour and salt; beat in gradually on low speed just until blended. Stir in vanilla.

2 Pour batter into a greased and floured 10" Bundt® pan. Bake at 300 degrees for one hour and 40 minutes, or until a toothpick tests clean. Cool cake in pan on a wire rack 10 to 15 minutes. Turn out of pan onto rack; cool completely. If desired, sprinkle with powdered sugar or drizzle with a powdered sugar glaze.

Serves 15

- 1-1/2 c. butter, softened
- 8-oz. pkg. cream cheese, softened
- 3 c. sugar
- 6 eggs
- 3 c. all-purpose flour
- 1/8 t. salt
- 1 T. vanilla extract
- Optional: powdered sugar or powdered sugar glaze

HOPSCOTCH COOKIES

**MARLENE DARNELL
NEWPORT BEACH, CA**

*Ever since my great-aunt discovered this recipe, we've enjoyed
these no-bake cookies at family gatherings.*

4 c. mini marshmallows

5-oz. can chow mein
noodles

12-oz. pkg. butterscotch
chips

1 c. creamy peanut
butter

1 Combine marshmallows and noodles in a
heat-proof bowl; set aside. In a double boiler over
medium heat, melt together butterscotch chips
and peanut butter. Pour butterscotch mixture over
marshmallow mixture. Stir until marshmallows are
slightly melted. Drop by teaspoonfuls onto wax
paper-lined baking sheets. Refrigerate at
least 15 minutes before serving.

Makes 4 to 5 dozen

JUDY'S BROWNIE COOKIES

**JUDY BORECKY
ESCONDIDO, CA**

*My husband loves these cookies...and who wouldn't, with chocolate
chips, cranberries and crunchy oats?*

20-oz. pkg. brownie mix

1-1/2 c. quick-cooking
oats, uncooked

1/2 c. oil

2 eggs, beaten

1/2 c. semi-sweet
chocolate chips

1/2 c. sweetened dried
cranberries

Optional: pecan halves

1 In a large bowl, combine dry brownie mix, oats,
oil and eggs; mix well. Stir in chocolate chips and
cranberries. Drop dough by rounded teaspoons onto
ungreased baking sheets. If desired, press 3 to
4 pecan halves onto the top of each cookie. Bake,
one sheet at a time, at 350 degrees for 15 to
17 minutes. Let cookies cool for 2 minutes; remove
to wire racks and cool completely.

Makes 2 dozen

HOT MILK SPONGE CAKE

CHERYL VOLBRUCK
COSTA MESA, CA

In our family of seven, my mother always had something good cooking and the wonderful aroma filled our house. This was one of the first recipes I asked her for. It's a unique recipe because it doesn't have any shortening in the ingredients. The recipe was handed down from Mom's great grandmother and we would beg for it on our birthdays! To honor Mom, and all that she's done for us over the years, I'm sharing our favorite recipe.

1 Combine eggs and sugar, mixing well. Blend in milk and vanilla. Add the remaining dry ingredients and stir with a wooden spoon. Pour into an ungreased Bundt® or tube pan.

2 Bake at 300 degrees for 40 to 60 minutes, or until a toothpick inserted in the center comes out clean. To cool, place pan upside down over a funnel or large bottle. While still warm, loosen edges and remove cake from pan.

Serves 10 to 12

4 eggs, lightly beaten
2 c. sugar
1 c. milk, scalded then cooled
1 t. vanilla extract
2-1/2 c. all-purpose flour
2 t. baking powder
1/4 t. salt

JUDY'S SALTY-SWEET PEANUT COOKIES

JUDY BORECKY
ESCONDIDO, CA

While my husband and three sons were watching the Chicago Bears, they would munch on sweet & salty glazed peanuts. I tossed some into my cookie batter one day, and voilà, this tasty recipe was born!

1 c. butter, softened
1-1/2 c. brown sugar, packed
2 eggs
1 t. vanilla extract
1-1/2 c. all-purpose flour
1 t. baking soda
1/2 t. salt
3 c. quick-cooking oats, uncooked
2 c. sweet & salty glazed peanuts

1 In a bowl, beat together butter and sugar with an electric mixer on medium speed until fluffy. Beat in eggs, one at a time, and vanilla until incorporated.

2 In a separate bowl, stir together flour, baking soda and salt. Slowly beat flour mixture into butter mixture. Fold in oats and peanuts. Roll dough into one-inch balls and place on lightly greased baking sheets. Bake at 375 degrees for 12 minutes, or until golden.

Makes about 4 dozen

CALIFORNIA COOL

With all the California produce, residents get off the hectic freeways and find some good farmers' markets, which can be enjoyed all year 'round. Fruit is often served for dessert.

PEANUT BUTTER CRUNCH CANDY

PAULA STOW
CHINO, CA

Always a crowd-pleaser and so easy to make. It's a fairly soft, rich candy, so you don't need a big piece to feel satisfied.

1 Line a 13"x9" baking pan with parchment paper, allowing some paper to hang over long edges of pan; set aside. Place chocolate in a microwave-safe bowl. Microwave on high for 2 minutes; stir. If not all the chocolate is melted, microwave for another 30 to 45 seconds. Stir in peanut butter; mix thoroughly. Fold in cereal and marshmallows, keeping marshmallows as whole as possible.

2 Pour mixture into parchment paper-lined baking pan. Cool for 30 minutes in refrigerator, or about 1-1/2 hours at room temperature. Remove candy, lifting out by the parchment paper. Peel off paper and cut candy into one-inch squares. Store in an airtight container.

Makes about 8 dozen

16-oz. pkg. white melting chocolate, chopped

1/2 c. crunchy peanut butter

2 c. crispy rice cereal

2 c. mini marshmallows

POPPY SEED CAKE

PAMELA BENNETT
WHITTIER, CA

I have been making this cake for parties, showers, cake walks, fundraisers...you name it, for years! For a flavorful change, sprinkle the greased pan with cinnamon-sugar instead of flour.

18-1/2 oz. pkg. white or
   yellow cake mix
3.4-oz. pkg. instant
   lemon pudding mix
1 c. water
1/2 c. oil
4 eggs, beaten
1/4 c. poppy seed
1 t. almond extract

1 In a large bowl, mix together dry cake and pudding mixes. Add water and oil; beat well with an electric mixer on medium speed. Beat in eggs, one at a time. Add poppy seed and extract; beat until smooth.

2 Pour batter into a well greased and floured Bundt® pan. Bake at 350 degrees for about 45 minutes, until a toothpick comes out clean. Allow cake to cool in pan for 15 minutes before removing. Drizzle with Lemon Glaze, if desired; cake is also delicious served plain.

Makes 10 to 12 servings

LEMON GLAZE:
2 c. powdered sugar
3 T. milk
1/2 t. lemon extract

1 Mix together powdered sugar and milk to desired thickness for drizzling; stir in extract.

RASPBERRY UPSIDE-DOWN CAKE

MARIAN BUCKLEY
FONTANA, CA

Never a fan of pineapple, I did a little dance of joy when a friend made this variation for me!

1 Drizzle butter in a 9" round cake pan; sprinkle sugar over top. Arrange raspberries, open ends up, over sugar mixture; sprinkle with almonds. In a bowl, combine remaining ingredients except garnish.

2 Beat with an electric mixer on medium speed for 4 minutes. Pour into pan. Bake at 350 degrees for 35 to 40 minutes, until a toothpick tests clean. Immediately place a heatproof serving plate upside-down over pan; turn plate and pan over. Leave pan over cake for one minute to allow sugar mixture to drizzle over cake; remove pan. Cool 10 minutes before serving. Garnish as desired and serve warm.

Makes 9 servings

1/4 c. butter, melted
1/4 c. sugar
1-1/2 c. raspberries
2 T. sliced almonds
1-1/2 c. biscuit baking mix
1/2 c. sugar
1/2 c. milk
2 T. oil
1/2 t. vanilla extract
1/2 t. almond extract
1 egg, beaten
Garnish: additional raspberries and sliced almonds

GREAT IDEA

Surprise your chocolate-chip-cookie-lover friends with a treat they will never forget! Put a scoop of ice cream between two cookies and make an ice-cream sandwich. Yummy!

INDEX